Exploring
The
Human
Aura

EXPLORING
THE

A New Way of
Viewing
- and Investigating -

HUMAN AURA:

Psychic Phenomena

by
NICHOLAS M. REGUSH
in collaboration with
JAN MERTA

PRENTICE -HALL, INC.,
Englewood Cliffs, N.J.

For Bill Decker

Library of Congress Cataloging in Publication Data

Regush, Nicholas M
    Exploring the human aura.

    Bibliography: p.
    Includes index.
    1. Aura. 2. Psychical research. I. Merta, Jan, joint author.
II. Title. [DNLM: 1. Parapsychology. BF1031 R344e]
BF1389.A8R43   133.8   75-2304   ISBN 0-13-297036-8

ACKNOWLEDGEMENTS

I have to take full responsibility for all statements made in this book. The stimulus for the ideas, however, comes from an enormous body of work produced through the ages, and so I make no claim for originality.

The person most responsible for motivating my interest, however, has been Jan Merta. Over the eighteen months it took to research and write this book, Jan and I had a great number of conversations. His own strong interest in the aura and his belief that it served some regulatory or protective function played a large role in my choice of research focus.

The number of drafts I needed to organize the material were miraculously and cheerfully typed by my secretary and sometimes research assistant, Norah Lloyd-Jones, often at very short notice. Her good humor and professional spirit were a great source of inspiration.

As always, my wife June took time out of her own busy schedule, editing, offering comment, and ignoring my irritability when the days grew very long. Her own interest in psychic phenomena allowed for many exciting and creative discussions.

Contents

Man has no Body distinct from his Soul;
  for that called Body is a portion
    of Soul
  discern'd by the five Senses,
    the chief
  inlets of Soul in this age;

Energy is the only life and is
    from the Body;
  and Reason is the bound or outward
  circumference of energy.

Energy is Eternal Delight.

WILLIAM BLAKE
The Marriage of Heaven and Hell, 1793

The
Road
to
Danville

The tall trees of the Green Mountains swayed rhythmically in the cool September breeze. Far from the staccato of city life, the winding road to Danville cut through tiny Vermont river valleys, sprawling farmlands, gradually steering deeper into a tranquil, almost desolate world. My weekend stay in the tiny New England village, I hoped, would help me fit together some pieces of an extraordinary puzzle.

Two months earlier at Virginia Beach, I combined a ten-day ocean vacation with daily visits to the Association for Research and Enlightenment (A.R.E.), dedicated to studying the prophetic "readings" of the late American clairvoyant, Edgar Cayce. My interest in this enormous body of fourteen million words had been heightened by Gina Cerminara's *Many Mansions* about Cayce and reincarnation, and it seemed like an excellent opportunity to get myself more involved.

Edgar Cayce had discovered that while in a trancelike sleep, he could provide detailed answers to a wide range of questions. During his lifetime, he gave over sixteen thousand of these "readings" for people, and fortunately the A.R.E. had about fourteen thousand carefully indexed and filed.

Cayce had diagnosed some eight thousand health problems and recommended very specific treatment for each individual. Presenting the most uncanny remedies, including an assortment of wet-cell appliances, herbs, special diets, and spinal manipulations, Cayce had an almost infallible record when his health recommendations were followed systematically. Years before psychosomatic medicine, Cayce had stressed that tensions and strains were responsible for stomach ulcers. Each cell in the body, he claimed, had its very own consciousness, with which he clairvoyantly communicated. Health meant a perfect harmony of blood, lymph, and nerves. The body, he believed, was a self-healing organism. All it needed was a "starter." A healer's task was to start the body healing itself, and if its blood, lymph, and nerve impulses were correctly energized, the body would counterattack whenever its defenses had been weakened. But like so many others whose ideas challenged basic assumptions about human life, Cayce had endured great hostility.

The A.R.E. has slowly built up a membership of people from all walks of life who have devoted themselves to the enormous task of ordering and interpreting these readings, hoping to relate them to modern scientific and metaphysical thinking and employ their benefits in everyday life. For me, ten days of going through this body of information had been enough to barely scratch the surface.

After returning to Montreal, my head still reeling from the tremendous intellectual and emotional stimulation I received at Virginia Beach, I was confronted with another psychic puzzle. A television reporter interviewing me for a show on consumerism asked if I was interested in psychic phenomena. He casually mentioned that he was a "dowser," one with the ability to locate water, pipes, and lost objects by holding a Y-shaped rod. Once he concentrated on finding water and cleared his mind of any extraneous input, the rod would dip over the exact location of a water vein.

After a painting had been stolen from the Montreal Museum of Fine Arts, he claimed he had placed a detailed city map on a table and slowly moved his dowsing rod over it, asking himself the present location of the

2

painting. The rod dipped. In this fashion, he zeroed in on a neighborhood, on a specific block, and then finally a specific address. He added that he was able to visualize the thief standing beside the painting.

He looked up at me and seemed a little embarrassed. No doubt such a revelation had evoked ridicule many times. "Dowsing is a very personal matter," he continued. "It's an important part of my life. Even before I board a plane I ask myself if the plane will crash. My system is simple: If the rod dips, it means no. If nothing happens, I cancel my flight. My confidence in dowsing is growing, but I certainly don't expect people to believe me. If you want to see for yourself, go to Danville, Vermont. The American Society of Dowsers is holding its twelfth annual convention, and you can watch some of the world's best in action."

The most ancient art of divination by rods can be traced, however vaguely, to the Chinese as far back as 2200 B.C., as well as to the ancient Egyptians, Greeks and Persians. References to *water* divining, however, appear conclusively only in medieval times. German woodcuts depict miners holding forked sticks searching for minerals in the Harz Mountains. When the technique was brought to England in the late sixteenth century by German tin miners prospecting in seabound Cornwall, the term *dowse* (from dowsing a sail, meaning to lower a sail), began to be used in describing the rod's dipping action. A more exotic suggestion is that *dowser* derives from the Gaelic *dahmsoir* or dancer. The dancing movements of primitive ritual can be likened to the dowser's keen sensitivity to the earth.

Dowsing became more widespread in Europe during the seventeenth and eighteenth centuries, and was fervently met head on by notables such as Jonathan Swift, who blasted it as superstitious nonsense in a satirical poem, in 1710:

3

They tell us something strange and odd,
About a certain Magic Rod,
That, bending down its Top, divines
When e'er the Soil has Golden Mines.
Where there are none, it stands, erect
Scorning to show the least Respect.

Despite its critics, dowsing has managed to survive. Today in North America alone, over one hundred thousand people are involved in dowsing, many of them farmers who despite the geological advances of a super technological era, revert to the old practice of locating wells with a forked stick.

Dowsing has even been used by Marine Corps engineers to detect tunnels, mines and booby traps in Indochina. Louis Matacia, an operations analyst at the Marine Corps Schools at Quantico, Virginia, initiated this activity by first demonstrating his dowsing talents to skeptical colleagues. Determined to convince the marines that dowsing could be used for practical purposes, he wrote a series of letters to high-level officers, including General Westmoreland, enclosing specific instructions for making and using wire rods cut from coat hangers. Eventually Matacia received word from Westmoreland's staff that marines were discovering all sorts of objects by dowsing, including Viet Cong food and secret messages enclosed in bamboo tubes.

Hanson Baldwin, a *New York Times* military reporter, wrote a story about Camp Pendleton marines who were waiting to go to Vietnam. They were being instructed to dowse, he claimed, by the commanding officer of the 13th Engineer Battalion of the Fifth Marine Division.

I had decided to drive to Danville to have a look for myself. What really baffled me was the television reporter's claim that he could dowse to locate a stolen painting from a distance of over five miles—or, for that matter, answer very specific personal questions.

4

As the road signs led me on to Danville, the autumn landscape brought back memories of my childhood. I remembered how I would watch the sun, moon, and stars play their game of musical chairs and feel the vibrant sounds of the universe flowing through my body. Years of growing detachment from the simple wonders of a child's imagination left me unprepared for the awesome sense of excitement that had been first generated at Virginia Beach.

For several moments, the road to Danville became a very personal path. I sensed each turn bringing me closer to a strong commitment—a psychic odyssey that would deeply affect my life.

As I approached the flickering lights of the tiny village, I wondered what Edgar Cayce, the dowser, and perhaps all of us, had in common.

Part One

Chapter One

The Odyssey Begins

"I don't know how it works," concluded the old, sinewy-faced man holding the dowsing rod. He then shrugged his shoulders. A long pause indicated that his talk on fundamental dowsing techniques was over.

"I want to ask you a foolish question," boomed a voice from the back row. "Could you dowse the outcome of a horse race before it began?"

The old man slowly raised his eyebrows and chuckled softly. He had been asked this kind of question many times. "There are two angles there," he answered. "You're asking dowsing to tell you something that hasn't happened yet, and I don't believe dowsing can do that. But if something was wrong with a particular horse, for example, you could detect this by dowsing. Dowsing can be alerted only when there is a human need and not personal selfishness or idle curiosity.

"Since I have been connected with this society," he continued, his voice getting stronger, "I have seen a number of cases which bear this out. One man who was very good at dowsing for oil up in Canada got himself tied in with an outfit which took a large number of oil leases. The dowser got greedy, and the wells he found went dry. Good mental attitude is a basic and necessary factor in dowsing, and his was spoiled by his lack of objectivity and goodwill."

A tall, thin man had been nodding his head repeatedly. Now he stood up. "I hold that dowsing is a gift," he said emotionally, "and the gift was not given to me for

9

horse racing or for the stockmarket. I haven't tried horse racing, but my son-in-law asked me whether I could pick out the four stocks his broker had advised him to buy. I did it successfully. I know I can do it, but I don't want people asking me for tips. The gift was given to me to help people."

A burly character chomping on a smelly cigar seemed visibly agitated by these remarks. "The idea that you can't dowse and make money for yourself is hogwash. In 1966 and 1967, I positioned nine commercial oil wells," he said defiantly, looking menacingly around the room. "The very first one I positioned was for myself. I rated a hundred barrels a day and up."

The old dowser quickly interjected that even though a person could dowse successfully for oil, people were apt to get blinded by a lot of money and eventually lose their skills. "This is a hazard that we have to recognize and face," he said sharply, looking directly at the burly man who had already bitten away most of his cigar.

I remembered that Edgar Cayce hadn't tried to profit from his readings, even though others were given information which brought them riches. Cayce's own readings relayed to him that his gift was not to be used for his personal fortune. In fact, many who became successful through Cayce did eventually lose out in the end, and Cayce himself would get severe headaches if his readings focused on financial gain.

The old dowser bowed his head solemnly, signaling the end of the workshop. As people filed out past him, he looked up slowly, his happy-sad expression telling me that he felt his responsibility to maintain tradition had been at stake. Was a new type of dowser infiltrating his cherished society?

Huddled in Vermont's awe-inspiring mountains, the quiet, remote village of Danville reminded me of an eerie Hollywood location when I first arrived on the moonlit village green. Early the next morning,

10

dowsers from all over the country began to assemble at the green. When all the early afternoon workshops held at the modern Danville High School had ended, the "set" was crammed with hopefuls competing for the starring role.

John Shelley, one of the society's greatest dowsers as well as its former president, had died three months earlier, and the older dowsers were reminiscing about this man's extraordinary talent. An artist as well as a former industrial designer, Shelley had been largely responsible for the society's growing public recognition, appearing often on radio and television, to stress how dowsing could be used to locate water and valuable minerals.

On the green, several dowsers were demonstrating their ability to find underground water veins and calculate the number of gallons per minute. Others talked enthusiastically about dowsing lost persons, caves, and possessions, picking genuine signatures from forgeries, locating blockages in pipes and even lost ships. It appeared many of the dowsers, while generally proficient, had decided to become specialists, and the annual society meetings enabled them to exchange practical tips from their own unique repertoires.

A prominent and highly respected society dowser was Gordon McLain, Sr., a gentle man who spent much of his time at Danville giving dowsing instruction to beginners. McLain's forte was forecasting ship arrivals in Portland, Maine, with an ordinary dowsing rod. He claimed he had been doing this for about four years. Once, when giving a dowsing talk at a men's club, he was given the name of a fishing boat, the *Betty Ann*, and was asked to dowse its location. McLain kept turning around with his dowsing rod until he was certain the boat's direction was approximately south-southwest. He then astounded his audience by calculating that the boat was approximately twelve hundred miles away.

Another popular dowser on the green was Herbert Douglas. When walking around the bed of a friend with

11

arthritis, he had found two subterranean veins of water were crossing directly beneath the painful parts of the body. Out of twenty-one patients whom he later advised to move their beds, ten improved considerably. Douglas also claimed that a copper wire could be placed around and underneath the bed to neutralize "noxious rays."

Many people had brought their children to Danville, and naturally, a few of them were dowsers. One expert shallow-well dowser, had discovered that his young daughter could correct his dowsing judgments. When he drove in a stake, she became mildly upset and insisted that the correct spot was four inches away. He believes that, when dowsing, his daughter can actually visualize the water. Like other dowsers whose children are learning to find water and lost objects, he worries about how she will react to the skeptics she will inevitably confront. Children he stressed, are natural dowsers. As they become older, they may lose a gift that everyone can possess.

The American Society of Dowsers has some members who were once very skeptical. Ray Poppleman had been one of them. Convinced only after he had been involved in an oil deal when a dowser was used, he then worked closely with a dowser forecasting oil locations for five very successful years. In the process, Poppleman had become a firm believer in encouraging geologists to work with dowsers.

While demonstrating a great enthusiasm for their divergent skills, many of the dowsers at Danville, were very much aware of the lack of scientific and government recognition and support. Times were changing, they felt, but not quickly enough. They had read Sheila Ostrander and Lynn Schroeder's *Psychic Discoveries Behind the Iron Curtain* which documented that Soviet scientists had readily accepted the validity of dowsing. Study results indicated that the human body was sensitive to underground water, mines, electrical cables in and out of buildings, and the changing magnetic fields of the earth, not to mention the electrostatic and electromagnetic

12

fields of other human beings. Dowsers, it seemed, were somehow capable of making this a conscious experience, using the rod as an amplifier. According to author Christopher Bird's survey article on Soviet dowsing, published in *The American Dowser,* the society's quarterly, the Soviets were taking all of this very seriously. Over one hundred scientists had met in Moscow to discuss what has often been called "the biophysical effect," referring to dowsing activity. The Scientific Technical Seminar had published a resolution mentioning how this "effect" had been used to map geological zones, find subterranean ore deposits, water, and archaeological relics. This resolution also called for the U.S.S.R.'s Ministry of Geology to involve itself in dowsing investigations and for the Ministries of Higher and Middle Specialized Education to allow lectures to be given in this area.

Why did American scientists continue to be so negative about dowsing? For how much longer would those at Danville be viewed as eccentrics and crackpots? Several attempts had been made to explain to the Director of the Department of the Interior that the Geological Survey was in a strong position to develop cooperation among dowsers, geologists, hydrologists, and minerologists. Orthodox science would not listen, not even systematically investigate. The survey had traditionally declared that dowsing had no value whatsoever as a means of finding water. (This statement has recently been conservatively changed to "Dowsing and scientific hydrology are entirely different fields of endeavor.")

America was not quite ready for the dowsers, but there were also signs that many of the dowsers were reluctant to let the outside world in. Why hold a meeting in remote Danville? for example. Obviously, many were content to find their wells and lost coins and to let it go at that, claiming they were being led by a higher source of wisdom.

The old dowser who had given the "Fundamentals"

13

workshop was on the green. His deliberate avoidance of "explanations for dowsing" had reflected this non-scientific attitude. He was walking very slowly with his Y-shaped rod held firmly in his hands. A young boy followed, watching carefully. The rod dipped. "There, that's where there's water," said the old dowser. Turning around to see who else was watching, he showed the boy again and again how to walk with the dowsing rod. Grabbing the rod from the old man's hands, the boy repeated the method and smiled when the rod dipped. The old dowser watched intently. The lines on his face began to twist with every breath and that happy-sad expression on his face finally dissolved into pain and despair.

This sudden transmutation made me aware of my own psychic schizophrenia. My rebellion against the intellectual limitations of an academic and scientific career had not totally quelled a need to "explain" how things worked. Nevertheless, I felt that dependence on scientific method to validate everything prevented me from exploring the world through other methods. On the road to Danville, however, I had sensed that the intellectual paths I was beginning to probe demanded transcending a purely scientific understanding. The old dowser's pained expression reminded me that I had been championing all the shrill demands for science. In his world there were values and ideals, assumptions about life and the universe that had to be understood in context, and not abruptly discarded in favor of statistics.

But even so I soon grew tired of watching dowsing rods pointing to water veins and retreated to the small book display at the Danville Town Hall. As I expected, it was totally abandoned. I approached the booth, signed my name on a blank sheet of paper, made myself comfortable with pamphlets, books, and magazines in a corner of the large meeting room.

An issue of *Psychic Observer* devoted almost entirely to dowsing included a statement by Carl Schleicher, then

14

chairman of the society's Research and Development Committee. He broadly linked the dowsing response to the interrelationship of the dowser's magnetic field and the magnetic field of whatever object was being sought. Himself a dowser, Schleicher had participated in a dowsing research program conducted by the Utah Water Research Laboratory at Utah State University. Over one hundred fifty men and women were randomly selected, ninety percent never having dowsed before. Each person was told to walk along a specific path with his choice of dowsing instrument. When a dowsing reaction took place, a block of wood marked the spot. These dowsing spots were then scanned with a cesium vapor magnetometer to pinpoint magnetic field disturbances. Computerized, the data revealed that there was a strong correlation between magnetic gradient changes and dowsing zones. It was concluded that dowsers do indeed respond to measurable magnetic field changes.

The Dutch geologist Solco Tromp had previously reached the same conclusion, noting that a good dowser could detect an artificial magnetic field one two-hundreth the strength of the earth's magnetic field. However, Tromp also found that the dowser responds to static electric fields. This suggested that dowsing may be a far more general response to a number of different environmental influences.

Dr. S. V. Harvalik, chief of the U.S. Army's Scientific Consultants Staff of the Advanced Material Concepts Agency, suggested that water flow produces charged ions associated with magnetic fields and minimal changes in magnetic fields bring about a slight twisting of the dowser's forearms. The rod simply amplifies this reaction. Harvalik warned, however, that heart and brain activity involving magnetic and electrical output would also affect the rod movement. The "monkey thoughts" of dowsers, the extraneous avalanches of imagery (especially those related to fear and sex) produced a large magnetic flow which could invalidate a dowser's judgment. The old

15

dowser who believed that obsession with financial success could be ruinous, had spoken from experience. Science apparently confirmed him.

What puzzled me, however, was map dowsing, which didn't fit this body of theory. For example, John Shelley, is credited with successfully map dowsing a suitable house for the Jersey Society of Parapsychology. In 1971, on the Danville green, he held his favorite nylon dowsing rod and asked Douglas Dean, a prominent member of the psychic research fraternity, to move a twig slowly across a map of New Jersey. Each time the rod dipped, Shelley drew a line, and finally a circle, around the area where the lines crossed.

By far the most celebrated map dowsing was Henry Gross's location of wells on Bermuda while sitting at home in Maine. No fresh water sources had previously been found on the island. Gross's amazing exploits and talents were systematically described in three books by American historical novelist Kenneth Roberts in the nineteen-fifties.

Other dowsing methods were equally puzzling to me, particularly those involving a pendulum—a simple device consisting of a weight on the end of a string or chain. At Danville, I had seen dowsers operating with pendulums made of wood, plastic, and glass. One experienced dowser even used a feather attached to a thread. When the dowser asks himself a question, the pendulum begins to gyrate. One popular but arbitrary system is to interpret a clockwise rotation as a "yes" answer.

The use of the pendulum can be traced to a medieval magical technique called "the ring and disc." The magician held a ring suspended on a silk thread over a disc with the words "yes" and "no" written on it. After praying to a particular spirit, he began asking questions as the pendulum gyrated over the disc. According to physicist and chemist Sir William Barrett and his co-author of *The Divining Rod*, Theodore Besterman, an investigator for The Society for Psychical Research in

16

London, the French spiritualists modified this technique in the mid-nineteenth century. A pendulum was suspended over a wineglass. If it tapped the rim once, the answer was no. Two taps meant yes. A series of experiments by a director of the French Museum of Natural History revealed that the pendulum's movement was due not to conscious willpower, but to unconscious muscular activity.

This interested a group of French dowsers who began to substitute the pendulum for the forked stick, believing the pendulum would be a much more sensitive instrument.

I soon learned one crude and very old theory of why the pendulum works. Everything in the universe vibrates ether, making communication and interdependence of all things possible. The pendulum is seen as an antenna. The subconscious mind of the dowser contacts the vibrations of whatever is being sought. Some dowsers claim they can diagnose disease and prescribe treatment at a distance by concentrating on bodily samples such as a spot of blood, saliva, urine, fingernails and hair. They believe that these "witnesses" provide a resonating bridge to the actual body under analysis. In *Practical Dowsing,* a symposium edited by Colonel A. H. Bell, the first president of the British Society of Dowsers, I found the following practical medical dowsing test:

> The simplest way for the beginner to prove this to himself is to hold his pendulum over his thigh, when he will obtain a reaction for healthy tissue. If he then slaps his thigh smartly with his hand, he will find his pendulum giving a different reaction—that for damaged tissue. Continuing to hold his pendulum over the damaged spot, he will notice that after a short interval the reaction will begin to change and will ultimately return to that for healthy tissue. The tissue has recovered from its very temporary injury.

Further instructions for medical dowsing stressed the importance of asking the right question and acquiring a

17

good knowledge of physiology. Although a few dowsers at Danville acted as diagnosticians and even analyzed what foods people should eat, I had noticed a general reluctance to discuss these techniques openly for fear of disturbing the various medical associations. Like Edgar Cayce, these dowsers strongly believed that any disharmony with universal energies brought on disease and emotional disturbances—hardly the dominant consideration in modern medicine.

It was quickly becoming more obvious to me that a weekend at Danville only stimulated a flood of new questions. I felt somewhat irritated that each small clue to the mystery of the dowser's wide range of abilities only created more confusion.

The late afternoon sun had scorched many faces on the Danville green. Everything was exactly as I had left it, except for still more people and more forked sticks.

Across the green, a bearded man with a large crop of blond hair leaned against a bench. At a brief conference held earlier to introduce some aspects of dowsing to the television crew from Montreal, he had been introduced as Jan Merta, a Czech-born student of ESP. I noticed he seemed very annoyed, his gaze fixed on two dowsers walking with their rods. He recognized me and looked disapprovingly at my tape recorder and camera. "You know, these dowsers drive me crazy," he told me. "I tell them dowsing has nothing to do with the dowsing rod, and they don't want to listen."

I remembered one early explanation of dowsing was that a sympathetic relationship existed between subterranean metals and wooden rods. This had been generally discarded, of course, and in more recent times, attention became focused on the complexity of the dowser's extrasensory abilities.

"When I was here the first time," Jan Merta continued, "one of the dowsers told me that he could tell me my

18

age. This was the first time I heard someone say that the rod could do something other than find water. He then told me my correct age!"

Merta had left Danville wondering how he could explain this. At the time he was Bernard Grad's research assistant in Montreal. Grad's highly acclaimed work on a healer's ability to influence plant growth had coincided with Merta's interest in psychic phenomena.

"In one experiment conducted with the assistance of McGill University technician Bill Mundall," Jan explained, "a sensitive recording instrument was attached to a dowsing rod and another device to a muscle in my forearm. Both instruments were given electric current and connected to recording pens. Therefore any muscle or rod movement created a change in the current, which was in turn measured. I was blindfolded, and a vial of water placed in front of me. First there was a measured muscle reaction, followed by the dowsing rod reaction a fraction of a second later."

"You're saying, then, that the dowser picks up some kind of signal and the rod moves," I offered. "But what kind of signal?"

"Too many people in the psychic field seem to want quick and easy answers," he replied. "If you have time, we can go for coffee and I'll tell you how dowsing and ESP are related to my everyday life."

Over five or six cups of coffee, Jan sensed that I was really interested and gave me a fascinating account of how his interest in psychic phenomena had evolved.

He was born in the town of Stare Mesto, an important archeological site in the Moravian part of Czechoslovakia, which was rich in folklore and deeply steeped in mystical tradition. On festive occasions, members of his family would tell stories of the supernatural.

"I never believed that such things could ever happen to me," he said "But suddenly, when I was nine years old, I had my own story to tell.

"One beautiful Sunday morning," he continued, "my

19

grandmother Frantiska Huskova went to church, leaving me alone in the house fast asleep. When I awoke, the sunshine was streaming in through the two windows at the left of my bed. Feeling very relaxed and listening to the radio, I suddenly felt a strange glowing feeling throughout my entire body, a feeling which to this day I cannot put into words. My internal bodily structure felt as though it was rotating. I was sweating heavily and hanging on to the sides of my bed. This feeling lasted at least a minute, probably more, then suddenly it stopped. I had the feeling of being airborne, the feeling you get when riding on a merry-go-round."

Soon after this experience he compulsively began writing poetry—odd, because until that time he had been a very poor learner in school. "My teachers were always wondering what to do with me," he said, "I hated poetry, any subject for that matter, and here I was suddenly writing verse."

It was a surprise for everyone to see little Jan Merta suddenly develop an unaccountable enthusiasm for any kind of information and a special need to be creative. He held on to his secret, letting no one know what had happened to him that Sunday morning.

"I became a daily regular at the library," he explained. "I read books about the ancient philosophers as well as contemporary thinkers, books that I could never have understood before the incident. At age fifteen I wrote a poem that was unexpectedly published on the front page of a Czechoslovakian newspaper, *Jihoceska Pravda*, years later, on the day Valentina Tereshkova was shot into space."

From a backward, sluggish child, he had been transformed into an energetic, tireless learner. But only when his education had propelled him far enough did he really question what happened to him. Remembering the old supernatural stories he had listened to, he reasoned that there could be a paranormal explanation.

"My grandmother, an avid Catholic churchgoer, again

left me on a Sunday morning," he said. "I felt somewhat lazy, very relaxed and happy that I was alone. The thought that she would later return with scrumptious cakes for me had heightened my dazed, euphoric feeling."

Suddenly, he heard a series of strong knocks. He looked up. Under a table in the middle of the room he saw a huge bloblike black object, moving around the table legs. "The door and windows were shut, and I got very frightened. I covered my head with my blankets and thought that if I pretended it wasn't there, it would go away. For a moment I thought I was dreaming, and I pinched myself. I even asked myself what my name was. I slowly found the courage to open my eyes and throw off the covers. Through the windows to the left of my bed I could see people walking along the road. I didn't want to cry out for fear that this object would harm me. Instead, I fixed my gaze on the wall clock to the right of my bed and felt myself falling asleep.

"Upon waking, the clock showed that only ten minutes had passed. The black object had disappeared.

"The next time I saw the black object," he continued, "I was typing poetry. About four o'clock in the afternoon, I had a strange, ominous feeling. I looked up from the typewriter, and near the windows was that black object again."

It appeared to be staring at him. "Without thinking, I immediately jumped from my chair and ran to grab the object. But it disappeared as I neared. I climbed through the open window and looked for it."

"Who are you? If you are the devil," Jan cried out desperately, "and you want my life, take it. I don't want to be confused anymore."

He then noticed that the big crystal chandelier in the room had been turned on. His paper was torn from the typewriter, as though someone had made a grab for it. He became even more determined to find the answer.

"One book about mystical experiences I had casually

picked up to read," he said, "provided an interesting possibility. The author had described how a scientist was found dead at his writing table with his diary beside him. He had written, "The black things appear again."

Was Jan's black object similar to the "things" the scientist had seen? He felt that there was indeed an important connection, but couldn't pinpoint it.

Very shortly after the black object's second appearance, he had a peculiar feeling that there was something wrong with his thinking process. "I had great difficulty drawing any kind of geometrical shape. I also found that I couldn't conjure up a clear image of people that I knew, nor anyone else after seeing them."

Most people can visualize someone if they try, but Jan had a kind of intuitive feeling supplying him with information about a person. He noticed there was a deep blue screen in his mind which stayed even if his eyes were opened. Distraught but excited at the same time, he wondered whether he would ever be able to make sense of it. "Immediately on this blue screen of mine, a tiny bright point of light appeared. I suddenly felt that the answer to my question was affirmative. I then asked if the black object's appearance had anything to do with my age. I noticed that tiny points of light, like rays, began to move toward that center point of light on the screen. When I asked whether these occurrences had anything to do with my extensive reading, the rays of light moved closer to the center of the screen. It seemed that I was building some kind of bridge to the final answer, that the screen was some sort of guidance system.

"After posing question after question, I hit upon a basic and very old idea that man was an integral part of a universal order which demanded harmony and balance." A human being needed mental and physical balance; he reasoned, mind and body had to be developed simultaneously. Before he had seen the black object, he had been working hard on his schoolwork, enjoying his sudden outburst of creativity, but forgetting about his physical development. "This created an imbalance in my system," he explained, "which prevented my physical body from using my overpowering mental energy. I think this energy simply gravitated outside my physical body. The black object, then, was probably my very own creation, a physical materialization of my highly energized thoughts."

Both times, this kind of energy release occurred when he had been very relaxed. The body—as an envelope for human energy—may have been overcome by the force of a strong mental current. "I then realized," he speculated, "that if I had been successful in hitting the black object with anything, I may have harmed, even killed myself. Perhaps the scientist who had written about the black objects also had a very highly developed mind but had completely forgotten about his physical body. And perhaps after projecting this mental energy, he tried to hit it and succeeded."

Questioning his mental screen, Jan concluded that developing a strong physical body was necessary to protect himself from losing mental energy; he subsequently became a good sportsman, particularly proficient in fencing.

This conclusion was his first tangible evidence that the screen served to replace more traditional forms of logic. "I didn't need to mentally struggle with any data." he said, "All I needed to do was feed my mind questions. It became a trial-and-error method. For example, what thinking process do most people use in searching for new explanations? Usually bits of data are put together in such a way that the person realizes he has made a discovery. I did exactly the opposite. I would reach conclusions without adding anything together, and without understanding the integrative functions of the many pieces of the puzzle.

"If I took an engine completely apart and asked someone to put it together again, that person would have to know how each part functioned. Perhaps it would take

23

him a year to learn." But instead, Jan's mental screen steered him toward a total picture of the "engine" a comprehensive blueprint which he could use in understanding how the balance and order of parts created the whole. "Later I began to realize that to understand extrasensory perception with traditional logic, a person could get sidetracked for years, constantly testing to see if two pieces really did fit, whether a third and fourth could be added, and so on. If we look at the scientific method, we can see that time and time again the scientist goes to great pain to defend the way he puts a couple of pieces together before looking for other kinds of relationships."

Jan believed that what was being called "extrasensory perception" had to be investigated from a much wider framework than was generally the rule.

Religion, philosophy and all the specialized sciences had their own well-established ways of dealing with the pieces of the puzzle they had chosen to explore. He would have to totally recreate within his own mind laws which fit more harmoniously with a much more comprehensive order—a universal consciousness that the blue mental screen in his mind appeared to reflect. The task would be awesome because the screen indicated only whether or not he was on the right track.

For weeks he would focus on a specific problem and draw blank after blank. There would often be no movement of light points toward the center. "Lack of movement," he said, "indicated that a question was completely irrelevant."

People could agree on a particular scientific position, but if his screen didn't show any movement, he confidently felt they were wrong. "Traditional scientific logic," he remarked, "couldn't sway me unless my screen showed the logic was moving in the right direction. Obviously I wasn't the most popular guy around."

Later, when he came to Canada, Jan had an opportunity to demonstrate the intuitive flashes he can pick up about people. At the Parapsychological Association annual meeting in 1969, he had met George Owen—author, former Cambridge biologist and director of Toronto's New Horizons Research Foundation—and subsequently visited the Foundation several times. Once in an experiment, three women were chosen at random out of a group gathered at Owen's home. Jan was phoned in Montreal. Each woman simply said, "Hello, Jan, how are you?" Fifteen minutes later, he called back with a description of their physical and general attributes.

Out of 113 statements, he scored 94 hits. When he visited Toronto about two weeks later, at a meeting he casually picked out the sixth person to arrive as the third who had spoken to him and the tenth to arrive as the first. (The other woman was not present.)

When I asked him how he did it, he replied that all he needed was a first assumption which he could use almost instantly to build up what he called "logical categories of information." Using the mental screen in his mind, he had developed an ability to quickly "see" the total person and then systematically order a comprehensive "blueprint" for each person.

I remembered Isaac Asimov once saying that "intuition is a line of reasoning which you don't yourself follow." To Asimov this was intuitive because, "A man couldn't put down note by note his line of reasoning." In describing people, Jan believes that his "logic" speeds up very quickly. Emotional understanding builds up before a more logical comprehension. When given the chance to work backward, he can usually give a good account of how a subject's characteristics are related.

Jan was about to continue our discussion when he looked at his watch and remembered he had to participate in a special demonstration scheduled to close the evening general meeting at the high school.

I was planning to leave Danville early the next morning and therefore made tentative plans to see Jan again in Montreal. "We'll continue then," he said cheerfully, leaving me with a small table stained and soaked with coffee, an ashtray full of dead cigarettes, and a head bursting with questions about the truth and scope of an alien territory.

Chapter Two

The
Friendly
Feather

Almost three months passed before I saw Jan Merta again. I had been working long hours on a sociology text as well as co-authoring a book on the mass media and consumer manipulation with a close friend, Richard Altschuler, leaving very little time for anything else. Had it not been for my wife June's enthusiastic interest in psychic phenomena, I probably would have forgotten about Danville for at least another year. Soon all the books and articles she had read began to pile up at the corner of my desk. I have learned through experience that when fundamental root assumptions about reality are being challenged, there is no ideal halfway observation post for me. I eventually have to face the challenge openly and honestly, or try to forget about it.

I was also teaching two classes in the Humanities Division at Montreal's Dawson College and before long, I was bombarding my students with psychic research data. One morning I realized I had completely exhausted my reserve but was reluctant to turn off the valve due to tremendous class interest. I thought immediately of Jan.

He seemed happy to hear from me when I phoned and eagerly agreed to give a lecture that same day. His talk was quite general and repeated much of what I had already covered, but I learned that at least half of the students were more interested in the strong, hypnotizing effect of Jan's eyes and some were actually a little frightened that he would use some mysterious power against them. My dealing with psychic data in a low-key way apparently had not countered sensationalistic expectations.

27

After class Jan appeared anxious to continue where he had abruptly left off, and after five hours at a nearby restaurant, he was still going strong. After four subsequent meetings, I managed to piece together some of Jan's psychic talents. Only this time, what he explained was much easier to understand and I was able to fit it into the context of contemporary psychic investigation.

In January 1971, Jan again had been the guest of the New Horizons Research Foundation. This time he had brought a large, airtight Pyrex jar sealed across the top with a fourteen-inch glass plate. The quills of two feathers were joined symmetrically, forming a pointer. Suspended by a nylon thread, the pointer was free to rotate horizontally inside the jar without touching the sides.

For the experiment, a nearby sixty-watt electric lamp brought the jar's temperature to slightly above 80 degrees Fahrenheit. When the feather "mobile" in the jar was totally still, Jan stood about six feet away. Appearing very passive, he raised his right hand. The feather began to swing to the right.

He demonstrated this many times, allowing the pointer to come to a complete stop before he moved it again. He then turned his back to the jar at a distance of twenty-five feet and easily moved the feather in the direction the observers wished.

When I asked him how he had accomplished this, he shook his head. "You know," he sighed, "I never assumed I had the ability to move the feather; I had not planned to test myself for any PK [psychokinetic] ability." Instead, he had speculated that if everyone had an energy field around their bodies (which psychics have often called the "aura"), it could be possible for this energy to influence a small object. He reasoned that freshly plucked chicken feathers could also have this "aura." Choosing a feather from the right side of a chicken and another from the left side (to take advantage of positive and negative polarity), he concentrated on the mobile and approached it very slowly.

"No, it didn't move at all," he said, anticipating me. "I therefore assumed that if this energy field existed, it had to be produced or activated by willpower. So I sat in front of different chicken feathers for two months for a couple of hours a day. Not one moved. Finally I got so angry that I began talking to the one feather and cursing it."

Suddenly the feather started to flutter. "Even when I didn't use my hands to indicate direction, the feather moved," he said. "Moving my hand in the opposite direction didn't affect my mental order to the feather."

He tried other materials such as metal strips, rulers, thread, but found that he was only slightly capable of moving inorganic objects, and then only when the air temperature was about 80 degrees Fahrenheit.

During his stay in Toronto, he also participated in an informal experiment in which a dowsing rod held in someone's hands was made to move upwards a few times at his mental command. "It got everyone jumping," he said, "so we decided to try something a little more exciting."

An angle iron used often in dowsing had been obtained from the American Society of Dowsers. About three-sixteenths of an inch in diameter, and twenty inches long, the rod was bent at right angles so that one "arm" was fourteen inches long. The shorter portion of six inches was enclosed in a plastic sleeve. This sleeve is held vertically in the dowser's hand like a pistol grip, so that the longer arm or "barrel" is horizontal. Just a slight drop of the hand is enough to swing the angle iron to the right or left.

"The guy holding the rod was told to keep it as still as he could, while I gave my mental command to turn the rod," Jan explained. After a minute of battle, someone yelled "Look at the aura around the thing. It's fantastic."

All five people present witnessed the flow. The person holding the rod offered that the aura "was in the form of a circular cylinder occupying a space within about one inch from the rod. It was gray and streaming out from

29

the rod in a direction perpendicular to the horizontal position of the rod. It was brightest when Jan Merta and I were concentrating on the rod. It resembled an aura of the type which I have seen around an electromagnet." When Jan relaxed his concentration, the energy around the dowsing rod faded.

The following day, the pattern was repeated. Present was Douglas Johnson, the well-known English psychic who claims he normally sees energy bands around people, but had not been told of the previous day's experiences. He claimed that he saw something extending from Jan's hand to the rod. "It was like a fringe coming from his fingers," he said. "It was about the diameter of a piece of spaghetti."

Jan did not feel that these Toronto demonstrations were satisfying enough, but he saw his experiences with the feather, in particular, raising some basic questions about the nature of psychokinesis.

Russian experimentation has shown a relationship between bodily stress and the ability to move an object. Nina Kulagina, for example, has demonstrated an ability to levitate a thirty-gram ball and move the white away from the yolk of a raw egg floating in a saline solution inside a glass chamber. When she is about to move a small object, she concentrates fiercely, as a number of films clearly reveal. During a PK session, her pulse jumps considerably and she has been known to lose three or four pounds. Researchers also noted that during some of the tests, Nina was producing theta brain waves at four cycles per second. She felt strong energy in her adrenals and at the base of her brain; and according to blood sugar and endocrine measurements, she was in a state of controlled rage.

This is the emotional state believed to often coincide with poltergeist phenomena—characterized by objects suddenly flying across a room. Traditionally attributed to ghosts and mischievous demons, such bizarre occurrences have also been highly associated with young children who produce theta brain waves while experiencing frustration.

In 1958 Mayne R. Coe, Jr. investigated the effect of static electricity, a force he believed would attract and repel all matter, both metallic and nonmetallic. It was a force, he discovered, which affected small pieces of paper, hair, and needles. Coe, along with members of his family, also moved longitudinally creased strips of aluminum foil by moving their hands nearby. When temperature and humidity were low and they felt energetic, they were more successful. Since all parts of the body discharge electricity, Coe reasoned, the entire body could generate an electrostatic force. Studying Yoga, he fasted and learned a number of breathing exercises to gain better control of the bioelectricity in his body. Having studied marine life, he compared the powerful current moving through his body to the current given off by an electric eel. Allowing the current to flow through him by relaxing his muscles, he was able to move a suspended heavy cardboard box.

Coe had been in contact with Joseph Rhine, who was then investigating PK at Duke University. Rhine's interest had been sparked by a gambler who believed he could control the fall of the dice by mind power alone. Coe's experiments turned up an interesting result. After charging objects with his own bioelectricity about twenty times during an experimental condition, he had found that he became completely exhausted. The sequence of exhaustion, rest, and recovery closely coincided with the U-shaped performance curve that Rhine had discovered in his experiments.

Conventional thinking is that the person radiates or externalizes some kind of energy to the object, causing it to move. While there is little doubt that certain PK phenomena are directly related to an electrostatic field, Jan suggested that there could be a very different underlying explanation.

Once a feather finally moved for him, he was able to move it almost at will, though with varying degrees of

31

success. In the morning he had to talk to the feather for at least five minutes before trying to move it. "I had to be friendly with the feather," he said. "I needed to feel a contact with it." The color or shape of the feather didn't seem to matter. Emotional disturbance of any kind and certain physiological reactions such as sweating seemed to help movement, as did lack of body control (during illness and after drinking alcohol, for example). Jan also had to use a fresh pair of feathers every few days, or no movement would take place.

Contrary to Coe's experiences, Jan found that when he felt very much awake and very "fresh," it took longer to get movement. Significantly, his attempts to understand how and why the feather moved diminished his ability to move it at all. "The important thing I felt, then, was that I had to be at one with the feather, that it was *my very own* feather. When the feeling of attunement was very strong, I had almost complete control of moving it any way I wanted."

Two recent and controversial discoveries offered an important lead. Cleve Backster, a lie-detection expert, one day decided to attach a polygraph to a philodendron. When he poured water on the leaf, the results recorded by an ink pen's zigzag action on moving paper indicated the plant was responding, perhaps emotionally. When he mentally threatened to burn the plant, it reacted more dramatically. Further experiments prompted Backster to hypothesize that a "primary perception" exists among all living things.

This statement has invited considerable scientific criticism, of course, primarily focusing on Backster's experimental design. Critics unable to replicate the results have been uncharacteristically vocal. Fortunately for Backster's reputation, his challenge animated a feverish interest in plant research. Marcel Vogel, a senior IBM research chemist, for example has stressed that a process of building up a sensitivity is necessary to begin the communication process with plants (just as Jan needed a short time period to "warm up" the feather). Vogel also believes that a plant must be "charged" by a person in order that it become sensitive to thoughts and emotions and in Backster's case, once attunement with his plant appeared to be bonded, his instruments recorded the plant's reactions to his state of mind even at great distances. A certain empathy is needed and therefore not everyone is equally capable of eliciting response from plants.

A second accidental discovery demands that we re-evaluate our relationship to other forms of life. L. George Lawrence, an electronic engineer and laser expert, developed a unique apparatus for plant research, essentially incorporating biological rather than electronic sensors. Living tissue, in a temperature-regulated bath and screened by a Faraday tube which blocks all electromagnetic interference, picks up plant signals. A continuous low whistle changes into distinct pulses when a signal is detected.

One day Lawrence was trying to record responses from oak trees, cacti, and yuccas in Oak Grove Park in Southern California. Lawrence and his assistant were having a snack. The telescope used to focus on a plant was pointing skyward when suddenly the steady whistling sound was interrupted by pulsations. The *nonelectromagnetic* signals appeared to be coming from the Big Dipper. Subsequent successful attempts to detect these signals led Lawrence to speculate that information communicated *biologically,* possibly by extraterrestrials, demanded a reexamination of the techniques scientists are using to intercept possible signals from space.

Lawrence himself readily admits that we know almost nothing about this form of communication but this is hardly any reason to ignore the startling implications. If a vast communications matrix underlies all life, what does it suggest about the complex nature of our everyday practical realities? Several physicists, including Charles A. Musès, believe we have created an illusory distinction

33

between living and nonliving forms. What other basic maxims of life processes required fundamantal scrutiny?

Psychic researchers have been accumulating a vast amount of data, much of it experimental. Testimonies from individuals claiming psychic experiences in the growing numbers of psychic magazines, newspapers, journals and books, are becoming too numerous to keep up with. But unfortunately, few attempts have been made to conceptualize ways to dig into this voluminous material. Any such attempt, of course, would require a comprehensive integration of information into a focused but *flexible* model. It also would require some starting point on which a sound intellectual case could gradually be built.

Part Two

Chapter Three

The
Aura

Aura; psychic atmosphere; surround; garment of the soul; the sphere of life—these are some of the names of an often brilliantly colored emanation around the human body which has been written about and illustrated since ancient times. In Egypt these radiations were represented symbolically on jewelry and ceremonial robes. The Bible says that Moses' face glowed as he descended Mount Sinai. Around the heads of numerous saints and of the Buddha and Jesus there are halos. One of the most beautiful can be found in the Gothic cathedral at Chartres. From a view at the south door, the awesome stained-glass rose window on the north side forms a spectacular halo around the upper body of a statue of Christ.

Statements about this luminescence can also be found in early Greek writing. The works of mathematician Pythagoras, philosopher Democritus and the Hippocratic physicians offer examples. One of the first attempts in the western world to deal more comprehensively with the nature of this mysterious emanation can be traced back to the controversial sixteenth-century alchemist and physician, Philippus Theophrastus, Bombast of Hohenheim, known simply as Paracelsus.

Viewed as a charlatan by his critics, Paracelsus condemned the narrow vision of the physicians of his day, arguing that their medical practice ignored man's inner nature, which was infused with a universal spirit. He spoke of a vital or magnetic force, a "fiery globe" he called "munia," which radiated around every human body and which could be used to heal others. Belgian physician Jan Baptista van Helmont, Englishman Robert Fludd, and many others promoted the idea of a vital

37

magnetic force which could be influenced at a distance, but it was Franz Anton Mesmer, a Viennese physician, whose name became synonymous with magnetism—largely because his views were much less mystical than those of his predecessors. In the process Mesmer infuriated the medical profession in the late eighteenth century, but can be greatly credited with building the foundation for more scientific exploration.

In *Maxims On Animal Magnetism,* Mesmer wrote that "everything in the universe is contiguous by means of a universal fluid in which all bodies are immersed." This fluid was the all-embracing medium for animal magnetism, which he claimed acted in varying degrees on all living matter. Certain people were more endowed with this energy, and could use it to heal others.

Mesmer stressed that perfect harmony of all bodily organs and their functions constituted health. "Illness," he wrote, "is only the aberration of this harmony. Therefore, cure consists in reestablishing the harmony that has been disturbed." Magnetism, he believed, stimulated the elasticity, fluidity, and movement of the body. However, Mesmer dressed in silk robes, wand in hand, to supervise the treatments at his luxurious Paris clinic, the sight of patients being magnetized in a huge tub filled with water, iron filings, and a large variety of mysterious ingredients, further contributed to his inevitable defeat at the hands of the French medical profession.

In 1784 a commission was created to investigate his claims and subsequently ruled that "there is no proof of the existence of the animal magnetic fluid; that this fluid, having no existence, has in consequence no utility." The Paris climate in the Age of Reason could not tolerate something that could not be perceived by the senses. But in his defiance, his ingenuity, and in the great influence he exerted amongst almost three hundred devoted students, Mesmer had, as Jerome Eden aptly put it, "destroyed the sleep of the world."

In 1845 Baron Karl von Reichenbach, German industrialist and scientist began to pursue the idea of a universal energy. More than likely, he was influenced by Mesmer whose interest in animal magnetism had spread to Germany, but remembering the official witch-hunt that claimed Mesmer, Reichenbach attempted to present his work in a new light.

Reichenbach must rank as one of the most adept detectives of all time, ingeniously unraveling what personality traits were common to "sensitives." Facing mechanistic nineteenth-century scientific views, he knew his case had to be researched systematically.

Reichenbach, for example, wondered why some people had a great aversion to the color yellow. Why did certain people hate crowds and refuse to sit between others? Other individuals hated silverware, hot, rich, and over-cooked foods, mirrors, and even heat from iron stoves. "Their sufferings," he wrote in *Letters on Od and Magnetism*, "are the consequence of their hitherto unrecognized peculiarity in the sensory faculty. . . ." All these aversions were experienced by the same group of people—sensitives:

> They are so in the very depths of their nature a nature they can neither lay aside nor treat with arbitrary violence; and whenever their peculiarities have been taken for cranks and contrariness, their feelings have always been hurt. They have quite enough to suffer without that from our everyday world, which has never hitherto taken any account of them.

Reichenbach stressed that human life was deeply affected by these peculiarities, and much of his writing is focused on explaining how and why. He reported that sensitives could see "flames" emanating from leaves, crystals, the poles of magnets, even from brims and stems of wine glasses in which chemical reactions were taking place, as well as many other "cold bodies." He called this observed energy *Odyl* or *Od*, claiming it was a universal property of matter which, since it penetrated all matter, could not be isolated from anything, even if it did exist in varying degrees of concentration.

His experiments led him to conclude that there was both positive and negative Od, the positive very often proving to be noxious to a sensitive. Coolness and a bluish color was characteristic of negative Od and warmth and yellow-red of the positive. He believed that dowsing involved detection of positive Od because many sensitives reported being nauseous when dowsing water or minerals. Most important, people were Od containers capable of charging substances and other people with this energy.

Despite his attempts to convince scientists that Od was a natural force worthy of further investigation, Reichenbach often found himself the victim of ruthless ploys when he attempted to demonstrate work with his sensitives. "Whenever I began to touch on the subject," he wrote in *Letters on Od and Magnetism*, "I felt at once that I was harping on a string of an unpleasant tone. They coupled Od and sensitivity in their minds with the so-called animal magnetism and mesmerism; and with that, all sympathy was at an end."

Reichenbach's work emerged at a time when the Age of Reason was already being succeeded by a Romantic period. People were turning inward, and facing the irrational labyrinth of the psyche. However, the proponents of a more metaphysical and vitalist philosophy sorely needed clinical evidence—some solid foundation for the revolutionary visions. Reichenbach believed the lack of an instrument which could conclusively reveal the existence of Od was the major reason his work was rebuffed. Those who refused to believe had to see an all-pervasive energy for themselves. Until then, little could be said for sensitives accused of hallucination and suggestibility.

In 1908 Walter J. Kilner, a physician at London's St. Thomas Hospital, discovered a method to make energy around the human body more visible. X rays had already been discovered by Wilhelm Konrad von Röntgen, and

Kilner had been appointed director of the hospital's x-ray department. He was busy investigating the nature of emanations from the body and had discovered his instruments recorded three forces including heat. Expecting that the use of dicyanine, a dye, would enable him to extend his sight into the ultraviolet range, Kilner then saw a grayish cloud around a friend, which he suspected was the aura. Aware of Reichenbach's work and clairvoyant descriptions of this luminous body, he decided to suspend all judgment until more experiments were conducted. What Kilner was eventually able to describe in great detail remains a classic treatise.

After perfecting screens made of thin, flat glass cells containing dicyanine dyes in an alcohol solution, he was soon able to detect three main parts to this emanation. The first was a dark rose, transparent and striated band, varying from one-sixteenth to three-sixteenths of an inch, wrapped uniformly around the body. Kilner referred to this structure as the *etheric double*. The second part, *the inner aura,* began at the edge of the etheric double and had a width of two to four inches, also following the body outline. Its structure appeared granular and striated. The *outer aura* completed the aura proper. Beginning at the edge of the inner aura, it extended about four or five inches at the sides and at the back of the trunk, and was a little narrower in front of the body. Structureless and nonluminous, it also projected a great distance from the fingertips.

While there appeared to be a relationship between the inner and outer aura, the outer shrinking in tune with the inner, Kilner didn't believe they were manipulated by the same force. The rays which shot out from the body appeared to be projected by human will, while he suspected that the second auric force was completely independent of volition.

Kilner studied sixty patients before making any conclusive statements about his discovery. As a result, his detailed and cautious research provided several important

41

correlations between the aura's shape and health. When an organic disease existed, the aura was either absent or showed a dark patch—a fact often confirmed by clairvoyants. Anger or intense behavior correlated well with expansion of the aura, while depression and poor health had opposite effects. For example, the inner aura, the densest part of the aura proper, was much broader in extremely healthy people. Its contraction generally meant disease. This was usually accompanied by loss of striation and coarsening of granules in its appearance.

Affection between two people, Kilner observed, brought about a transfer of energy. Auras flowed outward and blended. The perfect form seemed to be represented by an egg-shaped oval structure. In contrast, during trance states, the aura almost disappeared and it seemed to entirely leave the body at death.

Medical reaction to these studies was at first very hostile. In 1912 the *British Medical Journal* compared his evidence with Macbeth's "visionary dagger," but nine years later the revised edition of his book was viewed much more favorably by *Medical News*. Kilner had taken great care to dissociate himself from the occult. In *The Human Atmosphere* he wrote

> *It may as well be stated at once that we make not the slightest claim to clairvoyancy; nor are we occultists; and we especially desire to impress on our readers that our researches have been entirely physical and can be repeated by anyone who takes sufficient interest in the subject.*

Oscar Bagnall, a Cambridge biologist, was soon able to verify many of Kilner's observations and provide explanations for some of his viewing techniques. He believed that the aura was perceived primarily by the rods in the retina of the eye, which function at night or in dim light. The cones, the retina's other sensory neurones, are for color and clear vision. Perhaps realizing this, Kilner had instructed people to avoid straining their eyes by concentrating too hard on a body's outline. According to Bagnall in *The Origins and Properties of the Human Aura:*

> Since the rods lie to the side of the center part of the retina, which is lined solely by cones and which receives the direct image of the object being viewed, it would ... clearly be an advantage to look at the object, if not out of the corner of one's eye, at least not by peering hard and directly at it.

Bagnall further argued that since the rods functioned more slowly than the cones, Kilner's observation that the aura did not usually appear all at once made sense.

In his own experiments, Bagnall used a better dye called pinacyanol and verified many of Kilner's observations. But he could not see the innermost layer, which Kilner had called the etheric double; and suggested that perhaps Kilner did indeed have some clairvoyant ability.

More recently, Shafica Karagulla, a neuropsychiatrist and author of *Breakthrough to Creativity,* reported that sensitives she was testing saw a number of interconnected swirling energy streams around the body, suggesting that the so-called "solid" material body was a *by-product* of these energies. Karagulla concluded that there is a vital field of bluish haze which is "the exact blueprint of the dense physical body." She describes this field's makeup as "created basically from seven vortices of energy related to the glands of the body and interconnected with the spine through the nervous system."

She also believes there are three other fields: an emotional field which appears in color; a mental field indicating a person's state of mind; and a causal field which represents the sum total of the other fields in computerlike fashion. She describes the fields as interconnected by transformerlike vortices. Energy exchange between these fields is continuous:

> If an individual pulls energy via one vortex and the rest of the body is not balanced,

aligned, and integrated, he can literally blow a fuse. What happens is that if he has energy coming into a system where other areas are too coarse and unprepared, they become stimulated in the wrong way.

Observations by Karagulla's sensitives pointed to an underlying belief basic to all cultures: that man's role on earth is to evolve beyond the material plane to spiritual perfection, via an energy-matter continuum. The aim of the yogi, for example, is to tune his energies to finer vibrations. This he does by awakening the coiled serpent fire, Kundalini, and in turn, each of seven energy centers called *chakras*. They are located at the base of the spine, at the base of the sexual organs, just below the solar plexus, in the heart, in the throat just below the larnyx and between the eyebrows. The seventh is believed to be at the top of the head, perhaps in the brain. These chakras do appear as vortices and correspond to the seven major endocrine glands (in ascending order, the gonads, Leydig, adrenal, thymus, thyroid, pituitary and pineal.) Through meditation, the yogi can slowly activate Kundalini's ascent.

The writings of theosophists have shed additional light on this process. The Theosophical Society was founded in New York in 1875 by Russian-born occultist, Helena Petrovna Blavatsky and Henry Steel Olcott, an American. Devoted to a complete exploration of science, religion, and philosophy, the society encouraged a number of gifted clairvoyants who described man's relationship to universal energies in considerable detail. Charles Webster Leadbeater and Annie Besant, for example, who after Blavatsky's death became directors of the society, have observed that these chakras could be seen projected about one quarter of an inch beyond the skin. The double's primary function is to absorb *prana* (a Sanskrit term for an all-encompassing vital energy), which is then distributed to the physical body. William Tiller, a physicist and metallurgist at Stanford University, has speculated that "the function of these chakra/endocrine pairs is very much like that of power receiving stations and transmitting stations . . ." Tiller sees a cosmic source providing information which is absorbed into the etheric body and then expelled by the physical body. Unless the chakras are properly tuned, however, we do not get maximum energy from our environment.

The main problem with much of this information is that it is based largely on clairvoyant testimony, and again, certain scientific methods for attaining information are demanded regardless of the increasing appeal of other cosmologies.

My own rather naïve experience while watching a dowser at Danville is an example of how unwittingly selective a witness can be. Walking on the green, this man held what looked like a long piano wire with an aluminum handle. At the end of the wire was a heavy pointer. I was told that this was an aurameter which had been used extensively by Verne Cameron, a well-known dowser. If held a few inches from someone's body, the pointer would swing in response to an invisible energy field. An emotional person would make the pointer respond at a much greater distance.

My first reaction was that someone was trying to hustle a silly gimmick. But I later remembered that at the A.R.E., I was much more willing to accept the validity of Edgar Cayce's views on the aura. Cayce had claimed to always see auric colors around people and had described the aura as "the weathervane" of the soul. But somehow I felt that activity at the A.R.E was more "scientific." At Danville I had let some arrogance get in the way of understanding the aurameter in proper context.

Unfortunately, I was not alone. One Danville dowser watching the aurameter demonstration turned to me and happily said, "We now have *proof* that a unique energy force exists." She had just read *Psychic Discoveries Behind the Iron Curtain* and was overwhelmed by Ostrander and Schroeder's description of a new Soviet technique which seemed to capture the aura on film.

Around the turn of the century, Nikola Tesla (who developed alternating current), showed photographs of sparks flying from his body, taken while he stood in an electrical field. Then in 1939, the *Journal of Biological Photography* had published an article by Samuel Prat and George Schlemmer, two Czech scientists from Charles University, who had photographed apparently electrical patterns emanating from medals, coins, and plant leaves. These, like so many other important discoveries, had largely been ignored. Then Semyon D. Kirlian, a Soviet electrician, saw a high-frequency instrument for electro-therapy being demonstrated one day. The sparks it emitted caught his attention, and he wondered if it was possible to photograph them.

In technical terms, one of the simplest devices Kirlian perfected is a condenser system bridged by two electrodes covered with a dielectric. The object to be photographed is placed between these two electrodes, and a high frequency power source puts out a current of as much as 200,000 electrical pulses per second.

After experimenting for years, Kirlian was visited by a Soviet scientist who asked him to photograph two apparently identical leaves from the same kind of plant. At the time, Kirlian was discovering that each plant had its own unique photographable energy pattern. Therefore he was extremely perplexed when photographs of these two leaves revealed quite different patterns. This mystery was solved when the scientist told him one of the plants had been contaminated, but that it was impossible to see this effect with the naked eye.

Vladimir Inyushin, a scientist at the Kirov State University of Kazakhstan in Alma-Ata, who has worked closely with Kirlian and his wife Valentina, postulated that the visible energy pattern represented a single unified energy organism which was very sensitive to environmental forces. And the physical body appeared to reflect these changes.

When news of Kirlian photography became widespread

in North America, it quickly emerged as a dominant research interest for many psychic investigators. The mass media blitzed the public with spectacular photographs of kaleidoscopic energy patterns around leaves, fingertips, and Roosevelt dimes. Research reports revealed that subjects who had used tranquilizers and pain-relievers usually produced more brilliant patterns. Alcohol seemed to work that way too; marijuana did not. Personality and sex made a difference in patterns photographed; faith healers produced smaller glows around their fingers after a healing "pass," while the glow of their patients increased.

After a boom of almost four years, Kirlian-mania seems to have finally peaked. Many extravagant interpretations of what it all might mean is resulting in a more critical appraisal of the entire technique. William Tiller has demanded greater caution and better experimental controls in electrophotography, arguing that all the halos peculiar to the Kirlian process remain quite consistent when voltage, finger moisture, photographic timing and the spacing of film-to-object-to electrical-source are carefully controlled. Tiller believes that electrical discharges created in the air space between object and the electrical source in turn produces blue and ultraviolet light, which exposes the film. The differences in the halo can be attributed to the many ways that this light is influenced by physical factors such as finger moisture and spacing.

While this kind of constructive criticism has somewhat deflated many researchers' enthusiasm, by no means has it curbed hopes for an ultimate breakthrough of revolutionary scope. Throughout recent literature is the underlying expectation that a further exploration of man's energy field will reveal that the aura holds the answers to a wide variety of psychic phenomena. Better designed instruments, no doubt, will provide a number of spectacular revelations. But equally vital and fascinating research and theoretical paths to explore are also directly related to the scientific quest to capture the enigmatic aura.

Little did I know that a particular event at Danville would provide a number of important clues which vividly came to life only after I had closely examined all the background material on the aura.

Chapter Four

Energy
and
Information

Since that weekend I spent watching the Danville dowsers, I have become much more aware of just how tenuous realities can really become. One simple way to experience this is to drop everything you routinely do, if only for a day. Find some quiet countryside and allow your thoughts to blend with a brilliant evening sky. Become a child again for a few fleeting moments, and ask yourself what the years have added to your everyday perceptions. As you return home, try to notice the way your feelings and mental images become transmuted into more recognizable and well-reinforced patterns.

Driving home from Danville, the mountains soon blended back into concrete. Months later I was able to retrieve the images, but the hard-edged realities had worn away. What stood out in my mind most clearly was the claim that pendulum dowsing could be used to medically diagnose. Every part of the body was seen as vibrating its own energy, and the dowser's subconscious mind could *read* these vibrations. It was traditionally believed that an etheric, gridlike universe made communication and interdependence possible. The pendulum, used as an antenna, amplified these vibrations.

Today, physicists have largely substituted electromagnetism for a universal ether. Soviet scientist A. S. Pressman, for example, believes electromagnetic fields are informational. In this light, in an article prepared for a symposium sponsored by The Academy of Parapsychology and Medicine, "The Dimensions of Healing," William Tiller wrote:

> *Information content ... can be in the form of physical order or organization of a structure or entity, or it can be in the form of knowledge (a different kind of organization). Thus, as an organism grows, it ingests chemicals in a disorganized array and transforms them into an ordered arrangement in its own structured body. Higher organisms do the same sort of thing with mental concepts or ideas to produce a conscious organization of knowledge.*

Somehow the diagnosing dowser was quickly translating bodily information into organized knowledge. He was detecting a *lack* of bodily organization that reflected a state of illness.

Food can also be viewed as information, having its own vibratory rate and adding to the body's level of organization. One dowser had demonstrated whether a particular fruit had an appropriate energy quality for a person. He used a simple-looking device called a *biometer*, developed by André Bovis, a Frenchman well-known for his controversial claim that the shape of the Great Cheops Pyramid on Egypt's Giza plateau mummifies dead animals. It consists of a centimeter ruler with a moving slide and is used with a pendulum to detect vitality. Food is placed at one end of the ruler, and a pendulum is allowed to swing along its length. The point at which the pendulum swings back marks the degree of radiation quality.

The biometer, however, is only one means of amplifying the dowsing response. There is far more startling equipment called radionic devices. T. Galen Hieronymous, an electrical engineer, for example, has referred to an *eloptic* energy which he believes does not obey all the laws of electricity or of optics. He claims this energy radiates from everything in the material universe; that every element gives off a unique frequency as does each body cell. The vitality of food, plants, soil, and human

50

tissue, he claims, can be determined by noting the intensity of radiation with the aid of an amplification device.

Especially noteworthy about the basic device Hieronymous has developed is that the operator's mind is central to the process. In fact, the device seems to operate very similarly to a pendulum. The operator asks himself questions about the item under analysis in the same way a dowser does. If it is a blood sample of someone two hundred miles away, it is believed the sample acts as a resonating bridge to the actual body.

Hieronymous believes that just as a photograph can hold all the emanations of the object photographed, so can a blood sample, an article of clothing, urine and even perspiration. Each molecule of matter is seen as uniquely electrically charged and acting as a small broadcasting station which can receive and transmit. The charged-up molecules seem to build up a unique individual pattern, giving each person a very individualized "test pattern."

The aim of the operator is to "tune" the frequency dials on the device to correspond to the particular broadcasting frequencies of the sample. Like the dowser whose rod dips when a signal is being received, the operator of this device (and others similar to it, which have been developed in England) knows when the sample frequency corresponds with the device's and is therefore "answering" his question when his fingers stroking a small plate on the device "stick."

The fact that the device helps to focus the operator's attention on the task was borne out by a detailed report by the late John G. Campbell, former editor of *Astounding Science Fiction* magazine, who decided to conduct his own investigation of these claims. A circuit diagram of the Hieronymous device drawn in India ink seemed to work just as well. Here we see a fascinating parallel to Cayce's ability to "read" someone's generic frequency pattern and prescribe treatment to correct disharmony without using any amplifying device.

Scientists have always been very suspicious of mysterious energies, because history is full of ingenious frauds and eccentric inventors who often got completely carried away by spurious evidence. Other reasons are more subtle. Scientists work with paradigms, universally accepted theoretical predispositions which do not allow for sudden revolutionary changes to fit new data. Like everyone else, scientists enjoy occasional trips to the "countryside" but are similarly pressured to return to their everyday practical realities.

As a result of the recent explosion of interest in Kirlian photography, an important theoretical treatise first presented by embryologist Harold Saxton Burr and philosopher F. S. C. Northrup in 1935 has been ripped from its cobwebs. Burr and Northrup stressed that "each and every biological system seems to possess a dynamic 'wholeness,' the maintenance of whose integrity is a necessity of continued organic existence." They reasoned that the chemical interchanges going on in the atoms and molecules of all living things required an explanatory field theory.

"Field" is a term Michael Faraday and James Maxwell began using in the nineteenth century as a way of describing the emanations surrounding electrically charged particles. In particle physics, which is used to explore nonliving matter, a supplementary field physics became a growing necessity. It seemed, then, that organic matter did as well. A "field," according to Burr and Northrup, was needed to regulate normal maintenance and growth. They then concluded:

> The pattern or organization of any biological system is established by a complex electro-dynamic field, which is in part determined by its atomic physico-chemical components and which in part determines the behaviour and orientation of those components. This field is electrical in the physical sense and by its properties it relates the entities of the biological system in a characteristic pattern and is itself in part a result of the ex-

istence of those entities. It determines and is determined by the components. More than establishing pattern, it must maintain pattern in the midst of a physico-chemical flux. Therefore, it must regulate and control living things it must be the mechanism the outcome of whose activity is "wholeness," organization and continuity. . . . (Roman added)

Later Burr wrote that all living matter—even a tiny seed—is surrounded and directed by an electrodynamic field which mediates cosmic input. Using a micro-voltmeter he helped to develop which was able to measure electrical current as minute as a millionth of a volt between points on a living organism, Burr was able to show that abnormal voltage patterns could be detected before disease symptoms, such as malignancies, showed up in the physical body. Leonard Ravitz, one of Burr's students and colleagues, later demonstrated that the electrical potential found between his patients' heads and chests closely paralleled seasonal lunar fluctuations and that the depth of hypnosis could be detected by a voltemeter. Apparently a person's mental state affects the electrical patterns in the organizing field.

Biologists have resisted the idea that prephysical organizing force fields exist, even though they have had great difficulty in explaining the mechanism of energy distribution in the body. Jacques Monod, a prominent scientist and Nobel Prize winner who is also director of the prestigious Pasteur Institute in Paris, for example, has argued in *Chance and Necessity* that a physicochemical explanation goes a long way in explaining biological self-construction and self-replication. He has claimed there is sufficient evidence that the human species is nothing more than the result of chance errors in the replicative history of DNA molecules. The discoveries of Burr and Ravitz as well as current speculations about the prephysical body observed in Kirlian photography have at least cast *some* doubt on the principal theme in Monod's work that "God *does* play at dice."

In this light, astrology's age-old belief that intricate cosmic conjunctions influence planetary events and human behavior demands reexamination. A look at the effects of sunspot activity is a good starting point.

A sunspot is a cooler region on the sun exhibiting a very strong magnetic field as this spot moves through the sun's surface. A solar flare is a result of large amounts of energy being suddenly released, sometimes for as long as thirty minutes. These bursts of energy are now believed to be highly related to changes in human blood chemistry. A Japanese scientist, M. Takata, reported that great variations in solar energy appear to cause blood-serum irregularities in males. Nicholas Schulz and his associates in the U.S.S.R., after taking the blood counts of thousands of healthy people around a sunspot cycle peak in 1957 and 1958, concluded that there was a strong correlation between this solar storm activity and a general decrease in the number of white blood cells—one of the body's main defense mechanisms against disease. According to Anatoly Todshibyakin of the Institute of Clinical Physiology in Kiev, human reflexes become slower in times of peak solar activity. Even the number of traffic accidents increases, particularly on the second day of flare explosions.

To the late Russian historian Alexander L. Tchijewsky a quiet sun for the most part meant behavioral stability on the planet. Years of high sunspot activity in the eleven and one-half year cycle correlated dramatically with planetary upheaval. From 500 B.C. to A.D. 1900, Tchijewsky claimed, revolutions, wars, migrations and epidemics corresponded with the increase of solar activity.

Recent research by RCA scientist John Nelson has persuaded some skeptics to take these correlations more seriously. Attempting to clear up RCA's dilemma of how to avoid magnetic storms' interference with shortwave transmission, Nelson found that he could forecast with great accuracy when these storms would occur by plotting planetary positions. *Certain planetary alignments appeared to be triggering the unruly solar flares.* According to Richard Head of NASA's Electronic Research Center, if Mercury, Venus and Earth were aligned at right angles to the sun, solar flares would erupt. NASA calls this "gravitational vectoring."

The publication of *Psychic Discoveries Behind the Iron Curtain* introduced the work of Eugen Jonas to the Western world. Data coming from his Astrological Birth Control Centre for Planned Parenthood in Czechoslovakia, stressing the importance of moon phases in forecasting a woman's potential to conceive, as well as the sex of her child, has added another dimension to the steady unraveling of cosmic connections. Working with a claimed 97.7 percent success rate, we learn from Sheila Ostrander and Lynn Schroeder that Jonas has demonstrated:

1. *The time of a woman's fertility depends on the recurrence of the angles of the sun and moon that occurred at the woman's own birth;*

2. *The sex of the child depends on the position of the moon at conception.*

3. *Certain configurations of the nearer celestial bodies at the time of conception can affect the viability of the embryo.*

In a later book, *Astrological Birth Control*, Ostrander and Schroeder describe how Landrum B. Shettles, a well-known American medical scientist, who was one of the first to watch the union of sperm and egg under the microscope, has provided one important basis for Jonas's ability to forecast a child's sex. Shettles found that the male-producing Y-chromosome sperms, smaller and faster-moving than female-producing X-chromosome sperms, are less able to survive in the vagina's acid environment. But because of their greater speed, they have the advantage of fertilization in a less antagonistic alkaline-secretion environment, which predominates around the

55

time of ovulation. Moon phases, it seems, affect the alkaline-acid balance of the womb's secretions. Quite independently, Jonas has found, that if the moon was in the astrological sign of Aries, Gemini, Leo, Libra, Sagittarius, or Aquarius when the mother began ovulation and if the sun and moon were in the same alignment that they were during her own birth, the condition was right for a male child to be conceived.

Jonas believes that discoveries of other cosmic connections will enable scientists to carefully chart when unfavorable influences can be avoided. Even sterility and deformity may be related to specific planetary alignments.

The main implication arising from this work is that there is a curious clockworklike quality to cosmic activity and its effects on this planet, a perspective greatly shared by Frank A. Brown Jr., a Northwestern University biologist. Brown revealed that the crabs he brought to his University of Illinois laboratory maintained their regular twenty-four hour cycle of lightening and darkening their skin color when kept in constant light. When Brown brought oysters to Evanston from New Haven, he discovered that after two weeks of opening their shells at the time of high tide on the East Coast, they adjusted to what would have been high tide in the Midwest. The environment was generating some kind of time signals, which Brown believes is supporting evidence for the cosmic-stimulus hypothesis—the argument that organisms are dependent for their timing upon cues from the geophysical environment. Brown does not believe there is enough evidence that organisms have evolved internal biochemical timing mechanisms which parallel geophysical rhythms, and wonders why it would even be necessary.

Jonas thinks that cosmic configurations are part of an imprinting process, which corresponds with the beginning of human life. This basic cosmic vibrational impulse, the sum of energy wave frequencies at the instant of creation, gives the fertilized egg its unique resonance range and life potential. It has been suggested, for example, that accident-proneness may be heightened during the same moon phase which existed at the time of an individual's birth. The susceptibility for certain illnesses may also be related to the combinations and permutations of cosmic connections.

Students of astrology who have become overly fatalistic would be wise, however, to heed the words of medieval alchemist Albertus Magnus who said, "There is in man a double spring of action, namely nature and will, nature for its part ruled by the stars while the will is fine; but unless it resists, it is swept along by nature and becomes mechanical." This view reflects the ancient Chaldean and Egyptian belief that careful astrological interpretation enables a greater understanding of what forces stand in the way of evolutionary development. Alice Bailey, author of *Esoteric Astrology,* has similarly written: "As man evolves the mechanism of response or the vehicle of consciousness is likewise steadily improved. His reactions, therefore, to the planetary influences and to the energy of the various constellations change." She believes that those who do not consciously probe life's meaning have little hope of transcending planetary influences.

While all of the above data must be viewed as preliminary, at best, it is becoming increasingly difficult to avoid confronting a basic, old, and universal question: *Is there a design to the universe, a blueprint for our planet and for each individual? If so, can it be modified? And how?*

In his extensive investigation of radionics, Edward Russell has presented some intriguing speculations. He points out that while Burr's electrodynamic field (or L-field) is invisible and can be described as prephysical, it is nevertheless detectable with electromagnetic instruments. Russell believes that the fields involved in radionics are, in his own words, "pre-prephysical." He theorizes that the electrodynamic matrix must itself be preceded by yet another organizing field he calls a *T* or thought field. His reasoning is as follows:

1. *Thought behaves like a field and comes in an infinite variety of T-fields,*

2. *It can produce effects across space, which are not affected by distance or time.*

3. *Thought is independent of and can exist apart from the human brain.*

4. *It can attach itself not only to brain cells but also to any kind of matter.*

5. *It can influence the organizing L-field or the human body,*

6. *Organization, which gives everything that exists its identity and reality, must be the product of mind or thought.*

7. *Mind or thought must precede organization.*

Russell adds, however, that while T-fields "represent our varied memories and our knowledge, we should call nature's blueprints organizing fields or O-fields for short." He compares O-fields with architects' plans, while T-fields "are equivalent to artists' impressions."

How then, does the dowser or radionic operator "read" a person's bodily information? According to Russell, a rapport between the O-fields of patient and operator becomes established. Answers to questions then become translated by the nervous system. A "witness" such as a spot of blood is seen as helping to establish this rapport. Russell suggests that perhaps one of the main purposes of radionic treatment is to help bring the patient back into touch with the information in his own O-field which has become blocked by the wide range of everyday mental activity.

Can dowsing for water or minerals, also be explained by our planets' own information blueprint? Russell believes it can. "This planetary field," he writes, "can be

58

visualized as an inconceivably complex central filing system in which are filed all the plans, specifications and data which are needed to maintain the organization of this planet." Edgar Cayce's reference to the "Akashic Records" as the source for his own wide-scale information has a similar ring to it. *Akasha* is a Sanskrit word which refers to an electro-spiritual, universal, etherlike substance. Everything—all information—is seen as recorded on it.

Russell's theoretical focus, based on almost fifty years of interest in radionics as well as a keen appreciation of the electrodynamic theory and subsequent research by Burr and Ravitz, provides a formidable challenge. However, Russell is first to admit that this controversial explanatory system should be seen as a stimulus, rather than any conclusion, pointing the way to at least a workable model that can account for a wide range of behavior usually referred to as psychic phenomena.

Much of the research and theory we have looked at thus far suggest that the physical body is a transmuted by-product of subtler, prephysical fields. Man is seen as existing in "fields" within "fields." To see how long we have entertained this idea, we can go back to Pythagoras who viewed the universe as consciousness, and matter as a result of energy transmutations. Matter, according to relativity theory, can be viewed as a condensed energy state in space—hardly the usual way we see ourselves, but accurate nonetheless. Long before Albert Einstein gave us $E = MC^2$ (energy = mass times the square of the speed of light), the ancient Chinese viewed energy and matter as both a part of a single reality, a continuum. When clairvoyants describe the "aura," they often claim to see energies streaming into a person's energy field, which are met head-on by energies metabolized by the body, and a mysterious interchange takes place. Is this an observation of an *information* exchange? Is the "aura" an energy buffer zone along the energy-matter continuum? Is the "aura" a living computer, processing and transmitting raw information from the Universe to the conscious mind? In this sense, the body itself can be viewed as *organizing* information, processing new information. *Man is information!* The intriguing question is to what extent this information exchange can alter existing blueprints.

Chapter Five

The Telepathic Time Stream

I had met a dowser at Danville who spoke enthusiastically of her great fascination with Captain Kidd.

"I've read every book I could find on him. I think I'm learning about one of my past lives," she whispered. Her cautious tone suggested that she was sounding me out. Very abruptly she then snapped, "Do you believe in reincarnation?"

At the time, I wasn't even certain that I knew what it meant. The very ancient idea that a person's soul could continue its existence after physical death and then become associated with another body was a concept quite remote from my everyday life. In my reading, I had often come across it in Buddhism, Hinduism, in the writings of the American Transcendentalists, such as Ralph Waldo Emerson and Henry David Thoreau; in William James, Carl Jung and especially in the poems of William Blake and William Wordsworth. Leo Tolstoy's belief also had made a deep impression on me. In a letter published in *The Voice of Universal Love* in 1908, he wrote:

> *The dreams of our present life are the environment in which we work out the impressions, thoughts, feelings of a former life.... As we live through thousands of dreams in our present life, so is our present life only one of many thousands of such lives which we enter from the other, more real*

61

> *life . . . and then return after death. Our life is*
> *but one of the dreams of that more real life,*
> *and so it is endlessly, until the very last one,*
> *the very real life—the life of God. . . .*
>
> *I wish you would understand me; I am not*
> *playing, not inventing this: I believe in it,*
> *I see it without a doubt.*

I, however, did not see it quite so clearly. "I need much more time to think about it," I told the dowser.

Earlier at Virginia Beach, when scanning Edgar Cayce's "life readings," I had realized that a radical reevaluation was required of the great fear of death, ingeniously dramatized and perpetuated by North American culture.

All souls, Cayce had dictated while, in trance, were created at the same time in the very beginning and had been given free will to explore and experiment. Their destiny, according to Cayce, was to return to the "divine" by an informed, conscious and willful act and enrich the Godhead itself in creation. In *Venture Inward*, Hugh Lynn Cayce, the cheerful, white-haired director of the A.R.E. has described his father's cosmology this way:

> *As my father saw it from the unconscious*
> *state, the earth is only a tiny point in a vast*
> *pattern of what Man calls matter. Individual*
> *souls in spirit form, through the application of*
> *will in the expression of selfish desires, pushed*
> *into matter and brought confusion into the*
> *earth. Through the guidance of the Christ-*
> *Soul, the earth has been made a ladder up*
> *which souls may return to a consciousness of*
> *at-onement with the Creator. Through a series*
> *of incarnations in matter in human form the*
> *soul can learn to cleanse itself of the selfish*
> *desires blocking its more perfect understand-*
> *ing and to apply spiritual law in relation to*
> *matter. Urges created in the material plane*
> *must be met and overcome, or used, in the*
> *material plane.*

In Edgar Cayce's view, past experiences were not left behind but contributed to a multidimensional self. Cayce believed dreams could help recall actual scenes and memories from past lives, and that a person would likely dream of the personality drives and problems left as deposits by those lives. His life readings outlined how past experience had influenced individuals and what they had to overcome in order to fulfil their present lives. For example, a mother asked what caused the birthmark on her baby's arm and how it could be removed. Cayce indicated that by massaging it with an equal amount of olive oil and castor oil it would be prevented from getting larger, but he cautioned the mother that a "mark" was there for a very specific reason. In a reading indexed by the A.R.E. as 573-1F.30's, he said:

> Take individuals everywhere, where there has been or is a mark in the body and analyze their activity and associations among individuals; for their lives and their associations are different from the ordinary ken. Many will be found to have almost caused or averted tragedies ... in the lives of individuals. This is given her, [Miss Wynne] for many are close about her.

Especially striking and attractive to me about Cayce's cosmology was that reincarnation was not an escape hatch for tyrants nor for those who exploited others. According to Cayce, all people operated at full potential when their concerns were compassionate. Even more fascinating was his emphasis on the existence of multi-dimensional selves which clearly violated popularly held views about time. How could this concept be reconciled with a theoretical model which focuses on the way information gets processed along the energy-matter continuum?

The time categories still viewed as normal in our Western world are products of the Renaissance and Industrial Revolution. Clocks began to be generally used around the nineteenth century, although the mechanical clock was invented in the thirteenth century. Clock time is our creation and focuses us along a one-dimensional plane of past, present and future.

Before 1900 scientists considered space as three-dimensional and time as independent, uniform and one-dimensinonal. In 1905 Albert Einstein argued against an objective linear and unidimensional view. Time and space, according to Einstein, depended on the observer's speed and thus they became variables, aspects of a universal whole.

Time, when seen as subjective, represents our consciousness of change. We become editors of an ever-moving film which represents the informational universe. We ingeniously chop up this film into sequences of cause and effect. "It is impossible to think of the world, or of anything in the world," writes esoteric author and world traveler Paul Brunton, "without thinking of it as existing in time and space. This. . . is because the mind itself plays a most important part in predetermining how we shall see the world, compelling us to see it in terms of separate and successive images." Physicist Charles Musès believes: "We have a projection beam in our heads that passes through a set of images programmed into our projector and thus casts replicas of these images as large as life onto the screen of external reality." According to Musès, "we sit in the moviehouse of our minds like the prisoners in Plato's cave, suffering and rejoicing with the phantasms on the screen, forgetting that we ourselves have within us both the light source and the superimposed images." What we experience as time can be seen as that part of the "film" *that we have chosen to endow with stability and coherence.* The informational universe, like the drama projected on a spool of film, is timeless, but each individual carves out structure from fluidity.

One of the most articulate accounts of this process comes from Jane Roberts, an upstate New York novelist whose mediumistic information is provided by an entity who calls himself Seth. Because of its sophistication and clarity, it is especially worth considering here.

According to Seth, "Time as [we] experience it is an illusion. . . . The physical senses can only perceive a reality a little bit at a time, and so it seems . . . that one moment exists and is gone forever and the next comes, and like the one before also disappears." Seth, like Edgar Cayce, stresses that everything in the universe exists simultaneously:

> *Because you are obsessed with the idea of past, present and future, you are forced to think of reincarnations strung out one before the other. Indeed, we speak of past lives because you are too used to the time sequence concept . . . you have dominant egos, all a part of an inner indentity, dominant in various existences. But the separate existences exist simultaneously. Only the egos involved make the time distinction. 145 B.C., A.D.145, a thousand years in your past, and a thousand years in your future—all exist now. . . . Since all events occur at once in actuality there's little to be gained by saying that a past event causes a present one. Past experience does not cause present experience. You are forming past, present and future—simultaneously. Since events appear to you in sequence, this is difficult to explain.*
>
> *When it is said that certain characteristics from a past life influence or cause present patterns of behavior, such statements—and I have made some of them—are highly simplified to make certain points clear.*
>
> *The whole self is aware of all of the experience of all of its egos, and since one identity forms them, there are bound to be similarities between them and shared characteristics.*

Highly relevant to an information-processing model and a key point emphasized throughout all the "Seth material" is that the "self has no boundaries except those it accepts out of ignorance." An individual's energy blueprint, then, may provide the original stimulus orienting the entire organism in its selective pattern of growth. The growing child will not be fully aware of the vast storehouse of knowledge to which he has access. The child will tend to develop an identity or consciousness based on the dominant information that is metabolized in relation to his initial predispositions.

To better understand the basic character of this process, we can look at what is called *karma*, a Sanskrit word meaning "action." It is primarily seen as the law of cause and effect which applies to all human behavior. It is believed that retribution in the next life on the basis of present life activities finds its level of justice.

Karma may be seen as a result of the continuous process of energy transmution. Perhaps a metaphor here will help. If you take a drop of water from the ocean and then put it back, it loses its identity and once again becomes part of the whole. Take another drop out and it will not be the same as the first. However, if we assume, for a moment, that this ocean is the informational universe, this drop will possess all the information in that ocean. When this drop is isolated and then returned, it adds its individual quality to this ocean.

If we also assume that the universe is a hierarchically structured organism, being generated by laws based on energy relationships, the encoded informational quality of the drop that is placed back will be uniquely absorbed by the ocean.

Similarly, we are part of the "ocean." Certain knowledge is isolated by each individual's unique way of processing information, which determines how much of the informational pool will be experienced and what perceptions will be dominant. When the physical body dies, the information within its field begins its return process to the "ocean perhaps in some kind of computerized fashion." On the other hand, a new physical body also will possess all universal information, and its birth will be marked by a blueprint stimulus reflecting the total sum and matrix of energy relationships at that moment. Remembering other lives, therefore, does not have to literally mean remembering *our* other lives, but rather it might involve activating more strongly imprinted infor-

66

mation that we inherited. What Seth may be dramatically pointing to is our different levels of processing and organizing information, from the most dominant (what we call our identity) to other less activated "selves." An extraordinary medium such as Edgar Cayce may have been able to tap the more dominant selves activated by an individual. Other clairvoyants, less gifted, may be capable of interpreting only the most dominant self as it is being created. For example, the state of the "aura" that is *read* by clairvoyants, particularly by their instantaneous interpretation of its color symbology, may primarily be a stop-action view of the person's *dominant* self at any given moment.

Can this concept begin to explain precognition? Robert Nelson, who is the founder of the Central Premonitions Agency which records predictions, says that dreams the registry receives usually involve the dreamer as an observer, not a participant. In addition, a great number of the dreams that he receives involve passive scenes; the dreamer, for example, sees an event on television. A person here may be picking up an image from someone who has activated a behavior at some level of the self. We can call this activation a flow pattern. A correct prediction may therefore mean that this flow pattern eventually stabilized as it became dominant and physically real. A "miss" may suggest that a restructuring of the flow pattern occurred. Likewise, when a clairvoyant makes a prediction about a societal pattern, a "hit" may involve the ability to read this same process on a much wider scale. At one level, a keen observer of the physically evolving social structure in a society may be in a good position to predict occurrences in a so-called future. In the social sciences, for example, this kind of precognitive observation is common, and in fact, in many cases, is a foundation for widespread social planning. In effect what is happening is that people are setting in motion realities which in turn will be used as foundations for setting further realities in motion. What is processed as reality—that is, social consensus or agreement—by any particular society involves the stabilization of flow patterns.

Just as an individual through his unique manner of processing information focuses on one aspect of self and maintains this aspect in physical material reality, a society may be seen as similarly creating its history by building up its time dimensional reference points.

John Keel's *Our Haunted Planet* stresses that there are "window" areas on our planet, *i.e.*, places where peculiar magnetic faults exist. Keel points out that many of these faults are centered around ancient temple sites and areas where UFO's are often seen. In an earlier book, *Strange Creatures from Time and Space*, he proposed that many of the "monsters" and peculiar events which tend to recur in similar areas are due to these "windows." Another controversial mystery is the Bermuda Triangle, an area which stretches from Cape May, New Jersey, to the edge of the Continental Shelf, curving around Florida into the Gulf of Mexico and continuing through Cuba, Jamaica, Haiti, the Dominican Republic, Puerto Rico and through the Bahamas, finally pointing toward Bermuda. There have been numerous claims of strange disappearances in this area. A number of authors have proposed that ships and planes have been lost without a trace, and that at least one thousand people have disappeared. While there have been speculations about UFO monitoring of this area and that the victims are being clinically studied by aliens, there may be a very different kind of explanation.

The late Ivan Sanderson stressed that something was very wrong with *time* in this region as well as in eleven other "lozenges" which, he discovered, formed a trigonometrical grid "covering our earth like a vast fishnet of triangles with equilateral sides." Could it be that our physical world is also constantly involved in metabolic transformation in the same way as an individual's energy field?

Can the Bermuda Triangle be at a point in the planetary matrix which occasionally involves a highly unusual metabolic change? Can we also view what we call our human history in these terms? The books of amateur archeologists such as the controversial Erich von Däniken, and Robert Charroux dramatically report on ancient highly technologically advanced civilizations as well as the possible interference of extraterrestrials in shaping human history. However, many of the monuments, temples, strange drawings often featuring beings dressed in space suits, monoliths and underwater ruins may instead be serving as "windows" or remnants of other stabilized societies, now no longer dominant patterns in our planetary consciousness. *Does our well-reinforced editing of universal information maintain a time focus that prevents us from visualizing these remnants as part of coherent wholes?* Not surprisingly, the germ of this idea goes back to Plato, who strongly believed that the "real world" consisted of forms in which prior archetypal realities became activated.

Physicist David Bohm has described the universe as a complex hierarchy of small and large flow patterns. Particles extending throughout the universe give rise to larger patterns such as cells, organisms, and societies. Bohm also believes that these flow patterns can be restructured very suddenly.

This view is basic to an understanding of information processing. Each individual can be seen as differentially tuned to the growth of a vast informational universe. Our energy endowments, as well as our unique processes of individuation, regulate this information access.

Just as an individual is an assemblage of cooperative cellular functioning, so is a society (a larger flow pattern) a product of individuals. Just as the nature of an individual's information processing is contingent on patterns of energy interchange, so a society's stability and wide-scale informational processing depends upon the metabolic processes going on among individuals. Phoebe B. Payne and Laurence J. Bendit, in their study of

69

psychic communication, *This World and That*, give us one example of how this may occur. They describe how a person enters a seance room with an intact energy field which they refer to as the "aura" and how gradually a rapport is established between the participants, resulting in a common "aura," which in turn is disintegrated:

> *It is as if the individual aura lost its periphery, so that its content melted into its neighbours', but the essential core of that aura, the psychological ego, remained. Thus, at the end of the seance, when the circle breaks up, each ego gathers round itself once more the material which it has put into the pool. It is as if one imagined a collection of one-celled amoebae coming together and coalescing, so that for the time being one had a large protoplasmic mass in which the nucleus in each amoeba was embedded. At the end of the seance, each amoeba draws its protoplasm back to itself, encloses it in the rather vague film which is the cell-wall, and departs on its own business.*

Throughout the literature on psychic phenomena there are many references to the links that mold a society into a cohesive structure. For example, psychoanalyst Carl Jung referred to a collective, unconscious mind which was a storehouse of ideas, underlying concepts and human actions. Emanuel Velikovsky, the controversial author of *Worlds in Collision*, believed world catastrophes became embedded in the human psyche, and philosopher-mystic G. I. Gurdjieff referred to war as a planetary organic psychosis.

More recently, attention has turned to the communal "glue" which appears to stabilize an organic process, connecting everything else in the universe. This glue, often called telepathy, points to the cell-like biological cooperation between all living things.

At Maimonides Dream Laboratory in Brooklyn, volunteers were isolated in a room and asked to fall asleep. Electroencephalograph electrodes were attached to their heads and sensors to the corners of the eyes. An agent in another room concentrated on what researchers Stanley Krippner and Montague Ullman have called a "target object" (usually a painting), and attempted to relay specific impressions to the wired-up subjects. When Rapid Eye Movement (REM) a state associated with dreaming, took place, the subject was awakened and recorded his dreams. After a long series of tests conducted at Maimonides, while cautious to the very end about the results, Krippner and Ullman reported significant correlations between the imagery of the agents and the dream content recorded by the subjects.

These studies hold fascinating implications for what has become known as the sudden infant death syndrome (SIDS), long a great mystery to the medical profession. Infants generally between the ages of six weeks and six months die in their sleep, for no apparent reason. Doctors have theorized that viruses may act on the autonomic nervous system, triggering off a contraction of vocal cords and shutting off oxygen—or perhaps the lack of oxygen from a twisted head position causes a death spasm. But what is exceptionally curious is that many of these deaths seem to occur in clusters. Is it possible that a telepathic communication from a very sick child close to death may be picked up by another small baby who, since it would have little resistance to a strong telepathic impulse, may then die of heart failure?

Recently Soviet scientist S. T. Shchurin at the Institute of Chronic and Experimental Medicine in Novosibirsk in Siberia, found that cells communicate with each other by transmission of ultraviolet pulses of varying intensity. When viruses were introduced to a tissue culture in a sealed vessel separated by quartz glass from another enclosed colony, the normal colony was also wiped out. Perhaps crib-death victims are at a crucial point in a complex communication matrix.

In society, well-conditioned views of what constitutes reality remain strong when information processing of a particular kind is reinforced on a large scale. Philosopher Susanne Langer stresses that "nature" collapses into chaos once the fragile connecting threads of social agreement dissolve. Unfortunately the simplistic mistake is often made of equating political stability and "law and order" to a harmonious universal order. A strong societal flow form, predisposing individuals to process information in like manner, can't be equated with an ever-expanding informational universe to which each and every individual contributes in dynamic fashion.

How, then does a society generate a telepathic focus, thereby establishing some features of a past, present and future as more real than others? In the terms presented above, the current escalation of UFO sightings (for example) can be attributed to a change in the information matrix of the social "aura." For centuries, people have claimed to have received direct communications from entities from other worlds but agreements about UFOs have not been very strong until recently. (In fact, such communications are still generally attributed to madness.) But what of the numerous monsters often sighted, such as the Californian Bigfoot? The West Virginia Moth Man, stands seven feet and has red eyes and wings. The Loch Ness Monster, dubbed "Nessie" by Scottish children, dates back to the sixth-century; and what of the Snallygaster, that mythical, nocturnal half-bird, half-reptile reported to prey on children and poultry in rural Maryland? Are these other examples of human madness, or do they—and the flying saucer sightings—represent aspects of an informational universe which members of a larger society *sometimes* tune into? Do we for the most part, maintain a psychic agreement which prevents these objects from emerging as stable flow patterns?

Carl Jung believed that flying saucers were extensions of a person's psyche. Do they represent changes in the matrix of society, gradually transforming the collective psyche—a restructuring of the telepathic communal glue?

A recent hypothesis by Jacques Vallée points in this direction. Vallée describes how UFO's have been seen throughout history and consistently provide their own explanation within the framework of each culture. In antiquity they were regarded as gods; and in medieval times, as magicians; and in the nineteenth century as scientific geniuses; finally in our own time as interplanetary travelers. He goes on to say that the current tendency to accept UFO reports as evidence of visists from space travelers is a non sequitur.

> The phenomenon could be a manifestation of an advanced technology in a much more complex sense, involving, for example, interpenetrating universes. If time and space are not as simple in structure as physics has assumed until now, then the question, "where do they come from?" may even have no meaning.

Vallée concludes that the impact of UFO's in shaping man's long-term creativity and unconscious impulses is considerable. He believes:

> The fact that we have no methodology to deal with such an impact is only an indication of how little we know about our own psychic world, a commentary on the weakness of our insight concerning our own minds.

The work of Soviet astronomer Nikolai Kozyrev and Greek parapsychologist A. Tanagras on the nature of time offers an important insight. Kozyrev views time as an *energy* linking everything in the universe: "It is possible that all the processes in the material systems of the universe are the sources, feeding the general current of Time, which in its turn can influence the material system." More important, however, Kozyrev states that time has a flow pattern as well as a rate of flow.

Tanagras adds: "The fulfillment of prophecies is connected to fields of energies which humans direct subconsciously to living things or objects." What Tanagras may be describing is the processing and activation of multi-dimensional realities.

What is real to any one person may depend upon his own manner of dealing with his informational heritage and extending or narrowing his field. A society, on the other hand, may be seen as a transmuted information pool, an ever-changing vast energy product of a telepathic broadcasting and receiving matrix in which each individual plays an integral part.

Time, therefore, can be viewed *as a telepathic stream, its rate and flow dependent upon the nature of the ever-changing societal matrix. Each individual uniquely contributes to the rate and flow of this stream.*

Chapter Six

Healing
and
Cancer

On one of my frequent trips to New York, I had lunch with a friend I'll call Matt who, as usual, had a lively story to tell. He had read reports describing how Soviet researchers found that the supply of bioplasma often diminished as a disease in the physical body began. Matt had also seen Kirlian photographs showing the energy around a healer's fingertip being transferred to the energy field of the patient. In his typical adventurous and pragmatic fashion, he wondered what the *experience* of extending one's aura was like— and whether there was a technique that would allow him to do it himself. He might never have gotten around to it, however, had his fiancée not broken her wrist one afternoon.

"She had had her arm set in a cast," he explained, "but that evening her pain was quite intense. I had never tried psychic healing before and had no idea of how to go about it except what I had read. But in desperation, I simply offered to *try* to make her more comfortable. I placed my open palms over her shoulders, and tried to visualize healing energy coming down my arms, through my hands, and driving the pain out of her.

"I was quite surprised to feel a heavy tingling moving down my arms—very subtle, but something definitely there. But it was nothing to her surprise when she felt the pain ebbing! 'It works!' she cried, and got so frightened she asked me to stop."

Matt quickly realized, however, that this whole incident could also be explained as a matter of suggestion. "But while practicing on various headaches and tooth-

75

aches at the office, I found that when I placed my hands near an aching molar, say, the recipient always reported tingling and then warmth, usually in that order. Of course, normal skin can feel the heat of a cigarette up to a foot away, so it could be just the warmth of my hands they were reporting. But after a while, some people also reported *pressure,* as if I was actually touching them."

Matt resolved to put all three symptoms to the test in a way that would rule out any form of conscious suggestion. He would take a relative stranger who knew nothing of Matt's interests and simply ask the subject to stand at least six feet away, turn his back to Matt, face the wall, make his mind a blank, and report anything he might feel. "I was careful not to say *what* they should feel, simply that if they *did* feel anything, to let me know where." With this, Matt lifted his right arm, pointed to a specific part of the subject's back, shoulder, arm, or thigh, and did his best. "Now obviously there are a vast number of different places that the subject *could* feel anything," he continued, "and the distance was great enough to rule out body heat. So I figured any one-to-one correlations between where I directed energy and where the effect was felt would be significant. Also, I wanted to find out what sensations they would report, in the absence of any clues or preconceptions."

A good half of the time, subjects reported nothing at all. This was usually when they later admitted their minds were not at ease, or when Matt subjectively felt that his energy wasn't flowing properly. But when Matt felt a good surge of energy, and when the subjects' minds were relaxed and open, things were different:

"More often than not, the subjects would gesture to a point within inches of the spot I focused on. When I asked them *what* they felt, they invariably said 'tingling'! After switching focus, with equally good results, I told them I was going to hold the energy on that one place, and what did it feel like now? Almost invariably, the subjects reported first the tingling, then warmth, and then actual physical pressure—*always in that order*."

And just to ensure that their skepticism was shattered, Matt then taught *them* how to do it, and asked them to try the same experiment on him! "The technique is pretty simple. I imagine that across my shoulders lies a large, weightless tank of hot, fizzy Alka-Seltzer, under tremendous pressure. Down inside my arms run tubes connected to that tank. The palms of my hands, or my fingers, are the nozzles. I can either shoot energy from both hands, or send it out with the right and pull it back with the left, forming a circuit, which is what I usually do for healing proper. But for coaching purposes, I simply tell them to imagine that hot, fizzy water coursing down their arm and shooting out in a narrow stream to one specific point anywhere on my back."

Matt was happy to find that he could usually identify the place they were aiming at, "though often their focus wasn't too good. For instance, I'd first feel an *awareness* of one side of my body, which would slowly narrow to a smaller sensation of tingling. When the energy kept up, I *did* feel warmth radiating and pulsing there."

But how about pressure? "One guy, who was really loaded with energy to begin with, kept up his 'beam,' and abruptly I felt as if a physical hand were placed, very lightly and firmly, under my shirt, against my back. He was a good eight feet away, and wearing squeaky shoes, but even so, I looked back briefly to make sure he was still there. It's not pressure, really, it *seems* to feel as if a child had pressed its knee very gently against you: I felt the warmth and the imprint. And yet it was the *idea* of a hand that I actually felt, the concept of 'handness,' as if the word were made flesh."

Not everyone was able to make Matt respond, of course. But he found that when he felt nothing at all, the subject usually had some aversion to the Alka-Seltzer metaphor. "One guy said he preferred the idea of having a battery on his shoulders, and imagining electricity coming down his arms. I told him that was okay too, and as soon as he shifted imagery, I started picking up his energy with no trouble."

Out of curiosity, Matt sat down with one of his new pupils and tried a further test—one in which even *he* didn't know the answer. "As I said, I'm used to sending with one hand and receiving with the other. So I wondered what would happen if *two* people hooked themselves up in a single circuit, so that the energy would leave my right hand, enter his left, pass through him and back to me via his right hand."

Matt sat down across from his subject and held his palms face up, asking the subject to hold his own hands about six inches above Matt's, only with palms down. Then, on Matt's cue, both turned on the juice:

> The result has been the same in practically every trial I've done since. Very slowly, the "sending" hand of the pair on top begins to feel very heavy. Often it begins inching downwards of its own accord. The other three hands just stay where they're held. I then trade positions with the subject, with his hands below and mine above, and the same thing happens. Oddly, this kind of hookup usually leaves both of us more alert and refreshed than before.

One evening Matt was in a theater beside his fiancée, who had been complaining of chills and headache all evening. "I felt perfectly fine," he said, "and I really wanted to see the play through." But Matt knew her aversion to psychic Alka-Seltzer! "So I quietly moved my right hand into position and started zapping her for all I was worth. Now usually, in healing, I feel a sudden drop in energy flow when the subject has apparently had enough, and that moment came. But I wanted so badly to be sure that I had averted her flu that I started the charge again. As the second act began, I asked her how she felt, and she said, 'Oh, fine.' "

But by the end of the second act Matt himself had

developed such feverish chills that *he* had to leave prematurely. "I had the flu for a week, and the really disgusting part was that she did too: as soon as I drove her home, her own fever came back."

Matt's experiences prove nothing in a *scientific* sense. They are the kinds of experiments that anyone can attempt with willing friends, although as his last vignette indicates, there can be a danger. Matt understands this and has lately curbed his "healing" experiments.

A month later when I phoned him he told me that he was poring through a quickly growing body of information, both scientific and spiritual, which directly bears on some of his own experiences. It happened that his interest corresponded with the beginning of my own research on the "aura" and disease, so we agreed to meet again in the near future to compare notes. This meeting, however, had to be postponed, for a week later, after checking on a recurrent swelling and pain in my right knee, I was told that it looked as though I had a tumor in the knee and that an exploratory operation was necessary.

Facing the orthopedist, I asked the inevitable question: "What if the tumor is malignant?"

The tall, swarthy surgeon winced, then looked at me. "Then I'll have to cut your leg off."

When I was fifteen, my right leg had been placed in a cast. The doctor said I had experienced a "trauma" when hit badly during a high school football game. He paid little attention to the infection stirring in my lungs. Two days later, quite delirious with fever, I was rushed to a hospital.

The burning sensation in my knee was diagnosed as osteomyelitis, an infection of the bone with an abscess formation in the marrow. One doctor, after quickly looking at me, diagnosed the accompanying pneumonia just in time.

Since then, I have always seen physicians as very fallible. They made mistakes like everyone else. Giving up one's body, therefore, always involved a risk. Now, twelve years later, after the same knee had swelled following a casual basketball game, I had faced the man who had simply touched my knee and concluded that it was badly damaged.

"Probably a torn cartilage," he said. But after looking at the series of X rays, he was worried about the shadow near the knee joint. "The radiologist says it's a benign tumor."

"Are you sure it's benign?" I asked.

"Ninety-nine percent professionally and morally sure," he replied.

Happily, it turned out, I had no tumor—not even an infection—simply a torn cartilage! But I had been badly shaken by the entire experience. When I soon was ready to continue my research, I turned my full attention to cancer research and found an abundance of data which bore sharply on man's energy field.

Except for heart diseases, there is no greater assault today on human life. In the United States alone, at least 350,000 people die of cancer each year and almost 700,000 new cases are detected. Prognosis for most of its victims is not very encouraging. Four out of five will eventually die of it.

Cancer is generated when the normal process of cellular differentiation is disturbed. The double-helical structure of DNA (deoxyribonucleic acid) produces instructions which, carried by its messenger RNA (ribonucleic acid), tell embryonic cells what kind of cells they are and where they must go. Any minute foul-up as a result of viruses, radiation, or chemicals; whether in the living matter of the cell, the hormonal regulators of metabolism, the DNA or RNA or the intercellular communication control system, can stimulate the growth of fast-spreading malignant cells into tumors that completely ignore surrounding tissue. Normally functioning cells inhibit cellular crowding, whereas cancerous cells initially crowd an area and then migrate via the blood-

80

stream and lymph to other areas, where they begin clustering again.

In the late 1950s work done by Janet Harker, a British biologist, on the activity rhythms of the lowly but durable cockroach suggested that large amounts of certain hormones at the wrong phase of the circadian cycle could influence the rhythms of dividing cells. Dr. Mauricio Garcia-Sainz, working at the Oncological Hospital in Mexico City, has shown that cancer cell activity operates out of daily harmony with specific body functions.

According to two atomic scientists, John Gofman and Arthur Tamplin, mutations can be caused by natural radiation. Beta rays, X rays, gamma rays and alpha particles can break the delicate chemical linkage between atoms and electrons in human tissue. Atomic radiation and radioactive fallout can also be harmful to cells. Since all cells mutate at a low rate all the time, any sudden increase in natural or artificial radiation can disturb the entire cellular environment. According to biologist Barry Commoner, damage to a cell's DNA from radiation may result in imperfect duplication, but damage to any part of the cell can also stimulate malfunctions. He feels the cell must be viewed as a complex total environment. DNA is only one dependent part.

When cancer occurs, something apparently has disturbed the body's defense system: according to Dr. Philip West, biophysics professor at the University of California, we are confronted "with the possibility that all of us may have had or will have some form of cancer, but because of inherent natural control of this process, we will never know it." Dr. Robert Allan Good, President and Director of the Sloan-Kettering Cancer Center, has remarked, "In order for cancer to occur and persist there must be a failure of the immunological process. We never found a cancer patient in whom something wasn't screwed up immunologically."

While the body's defense system attacks transplanted

organs, bacteria and viruses, "successful" cancer cells somehow escape. Only recently has a strong but cautious conclusion been presented that the lymphocytes, known as killer cells, backing up the antibody immunity system (which also involves a complex group of enzymes in normal blood serum called "complement") are being overwhelmed by the amount of antigen cancerous cells release. Each cell, including bacteria and viruses, has antigens which are under constant surveillance of immune systems. Antibodies are produced for each antigen, but since each lymphocyte's radar system can only attend to one antigen, and as cancer spreads, more antigen appears to eventually tip the balance.

Radiation therapy is one of the most common forms of primary cancer treatment, basically for skin, head and neck tumors. But X rays can be incredibly unpredictable, causing chromosomal damage as well as inducing cancer in previously normal cells. Most drugs used to fight cancer have a similar effect, killing white cells and the antibody producing cells of the bone marrow.

When radiation therapy began, little was known at the molecular level about how cells were affected by radiation. In the late 1950s British and American committees formed to evaluate radiation effects even warned against diagnostic X rays because leukemia was seen as occasionally stimulated by this technique. By this time, many people particularly radiologists, had paid dearly. Alan R. Bleich in *The Story of X Rays*, describes some of the consequences:

> *The usual sequence was that the early practising radiologist would notice after some time that the skin of his hand was becoming cracked, fissured, red and inflamed. A persistent roughening of the skin would remain after the acute effects had worn off. In time, this roughening developed into a cancer. These early workers in the field had a succession of amputations, beginning with fingertips and extending through the hands, forearms,*

and arms. Ultimately they died from a spread of this original skin cancer to the internal organs. . . .

While interest in immunology is growing, a number of older and more recent studies are stirring up controversy. In France, for example, Antoine Priore, a sixty-year-old electronics engineer-inventor has been developing newer and better models of a massive machine which, assembled initially with spare parts from an American military surplus store, creates strong magnetic fields. He has been using it with apparent success to treat cancer in mice and rats.

One of Priore's supporters has been Professor R. Pautrizel of the Faculty of Medicine of the University of Bordeaux and Director of the Units for Research on Immunology of Parasitic Infections. Pautrizel suspected that the radiations of Priore's machine were stimulating the immunological defenses in the body. He injected mice with a blood parasite called trypanosome, responsible for sleeping sickness, and took daily blood samples after treating one group of mice with Priore's machine. He found that the trypanosome concentration in the treated mice was steadily decreasing, while control mice had all died after only five days. Thirty-six of forty-six mice treated survived with no trypanosomes left in their bodies, and mice treated by the machine before being injected again developed immunity to the parasite. These experiments appeared to vindicate Priore's own numerous experiments which claimed similar results with cancerous mice, but most scientists have not yet greeted this information as in any way conclusive.

Some forty years earlier, George Lakhovsky's experiments with plants showed that immunological systems break down when overpowered by stronger incoming radiation frequencies. Cellular oscillation would become abnormal, giving rise to faulty growth processes.

Lakhovsky believed that cells losing the strength to neutralize the incoming frequencies from microbes had to be revived. He used what he called a radio-cellulo-oscillator to supply diseased cells with correct neutralizing frequencies. In this way, the frequencies of electromagnetic oscillation in cells could reactivate immunological processes in the entire organism. Experimental work with plants confirmed this, as cellular activation attacked the tumor-building cells.

The work of Robert O. Becker of the Veterans Administration Hospital in Syracuse, New York, sheds some light on such claims. He has reportedly healed knee fractures and regenerated amputated forelimbs in frogs and rats by a weak electrical current. Becker, who has drawn significantly on the work of Harold Saxton Burr, attributes this to a "primitive system in the body" which transmits *information* to *all* of the body. He believes this is an electronic system and can be influenced by carefully manipulating magnetic and electrical fields.

While some work which may result in valuable benefits is still largely dismissed as "speculative," particularly if it challenges cherished paradigms, there is no doubt that medicine has made spectacular progress. Much of it can be attributed to the almost exclusive emphasis on viewing the human body as a machine, a reflection of the mind-body dualism expressed by René Descartes. Medical science, therefore, has developed newer and better methods to unravel and repair the body-machine's circuitry. In the process, the fundamental philosophy of Hippocratic medicine that mind and body could not be considered independently of each other has been greatly ignored. The tide appears to be changing however, and coincides with the greater recognition of psychiatry and psychotherapy and the interest in the powerful potential of the human mind emphasized in research on psychic phenomena.

"Mind is the builder," is a phrase that recurs throughout the Edgar Cayce readings, which related cancer to low vitality. In light of modern cancer immunological theory, this statement (made long before a difference

84

between benign and malignant growths became part of medical understanding) is enormously significant: "Ulcer is rather of flesh being proud or infectious, while cancer is that which lives upon the cellular force by the growth itself." Cancer, Cayce said, "was caused by breaking of tissue internally which was not covered sufficiently by the leukocyte due to the low vitality in the system." Although Cayce was reluctant to claim any hereditary reasons for cancer susceptibility, he did say that tendencies were probably passed on, that the kin of a cancer victim should attempt to build up their blood chemistry. For Cayce, the quality of thought was instrumental in all illnesses: "Anger causes poisons to be secreted," he once warned. In another reading he said, "Keep the healthy mental attitude, never resentment, for this naturally creates in the system forces that are hard on the circulation, especially where there is some disturbance of the spleen and the pancreas. An attitude of resentment will produce inflammation."

This next statement is of even greater importance: "Just as hate and animosity and hard sayings create poisons in the body, so do they weaken and wreck the mind of those who indulge in them." Poor mental attitude accounts for lower vitality, which in turn further affects mental attitude. This is exactly what Karl Simonton found as he studied the thought patterns of cancer patients.

Simonton, former Chief of Radiation Therapy at Travis Air Force Base in California, found a strong correlation between a patient's mental attitude and his response to treatment. While serving a three-year residency at the University of Oregon Medical Center, Simonton had been astonished to find certain cancer patients—all of whom exhibited a tremendous will to live—surviving against all diagnostic odds. Simonton believes that the failure of an immunological system is strongly reinforced by despair and a sense of defeat. He therefore tries to instill positive thinking in his patients. They are taught to meditate

85

regularly three times a day for at least fifteen minutes. Once relaxed, the patient directs his attention to the cancerous growth in his body and imagines his immunological resistance building and destroying abnormal cells. Is it possible that thought power helps block the kind of cellular death signals discovered by Russian scientists?

Simonton has also focused considerable attention on the ways relatives and friends view the patients' chances of recovery. If small globs of tissue culture can send death signals, what do whole thinking organisms do? I remember someone who had cancer of the larynx telling me that from the moment his condition was diagnosed, everyone immediately acted as though he was as good as dead. For this reason, a patient's family and close friends receive group therapy from Simonton. In this context, Elmer Green's account of Swami Rama's concept from Raja Yoga to the Academy of Parapsychology and Medicine is worthy of mention. Green, a biofeedback pioneer at the Voluntary Controls Program of the Menninger Foundation, has extensively tested Swami Rama's ability to mentally control his own basic physiological functions:

> The most potent of the various ideas of the Swami is that all the body is in the mind but not all the mind is in the body. This simple phrase has vast theoretical implications. The control of every cell of the body is possible according to the Swami, because every cell has a representation in the unconscious. Not only that, each cell exists, not only symbolically in mind, but also as a section of a real energy structure called mind. When we manipulate the representation of the unconscious, we literally manipulate the cell itself, because the cell is part of the mind.
>
> The second half of the phrase "but not all the mind is in the body" is related to the extension of mind into nature in general and accounts for parapsychological events, psychokinesis, psychic healing and all such scientifically impossible phenomena. The reason scien-

tists felt these phenomena are impossible is because scientists, at least the majority, have not been able to conceive of the mind as an energy structure which interlocks with energy structures both in the body and in "external" nature....

If negative suggestion may greatly harm a person's chances of recovery, a patient's reliance solely on others can have equally bad results. Giving up one's power of mind to others is akin to hypnosis. A person's immunological response may be severely weakened by the elimination of the important energizing quality of his own thought processes. While "healers" might be able to direct energy to an area of the body, suggestion of any kind may not last long if self-reliance is not part of the therapeutic process. This may help explain why some of the miraculous cures experienced at spiritual meetings presided over by charismatic healers are often temporary. Once the electrifying process of suggestion ends, the patient may lack the vitality to sustain health. (Perhaps this is also what happened in the case of Matt's fiancée, who only temporarily lost her flu.)

The late Ambrose Worrall, one of the most highly revered spiritual healers in the world, once speculated that "perhaps the spiritual healer blends his own field of emanations with that of the patient, resulting in a transmission of energy between the two." This has been somewhat corroborated by Kirlian photography. A healer's energy field it has been claimed diminishes and a patient's grows brighter and stronger. Ambrose Worrall, whose wife Olga today continues their healing ministry, believed that healing involved "a rearrangement of the micro particles of which all things are composed." Later, in an interview shortly before his death, he ventured that "the body isn't really what it appears to be—it is a system of little particles or points of energy separated from each other by space, and held in place through an electrically balanced field." Disease for Ambrose Worrall was "a manifestation of these particles being out of the health

87

orbit." It was healing power which brought them back into the proper planes—"back into a harmonious relationship." A person who is temporarily revitalized by a healer's emanations may again be overwhelmed by the same conditions which first stimulated the illness if daily life patterns are not changed.

The Hippocratic physicians believed in the great natural healing powers of nature. They stressed the treatment of the whole individual and not merely a concentration on his disease. A 1972 symposium called "The Dimensions of Healing," sponsored by the Academy of Parapsychology and Medicine at Stanford University and UCLA, was held to explore this basic tenet. The position of the academy is well reflected in the preface to the symposium's transcript:

> That man is a multidimensional being whose experience and ultimate purposes are inextricably and meaningfully related, and that that meaning is made manifest in patterns of health and disease. . . .
> The Academy also believes that medicine must [recognize] the unity of body, mind and spirit and the importance of the interrelationship of these dimensions in health and disease; that all physical and mental disease . . . must be viewed as a manifestation of conditions existing on subtler levels—whether mental, emotional or spiritual; that the treatment of disease must be directed at the whole man, and that no lasting healing . . . can be achieved where the mental, emotional and spiritual elements have been untouched.

The Chinese believe that acupuncture is basically a preventive medicine and that this vital energy should be balanced regularly, perhaps four times a year. An overabundance of vital energy or lack of it in bodily organs can cause disease.

Recently it was learned that the Soviets had conducted a fifteen-year experiment involving acupuncture, treating over ten thousand people in thirty-seven cities for stomach ulcers, asthma, constipation, and high blood pressure. Almost thirty-three percent were "cured"— almost the same figure as came from placebo studies, where it has been shown that sugar pills greatly reduce pain. Many critics of acupuncture have used this study to discredit its validity, but rather than view this as evidence for condemning acupuncture treatment, the results can be linked with the power of mind to revitalize the energy channels. Unfortunately as always in such cases, there is very little control evidence concerning what state of mind patients were in when tested for cure.

It shouldn't be surprising that what immunologists are finally discovering about cancer should apply equally to the dynamics and consequences of aging. Harold Saxton Burr found that the activity of the electrodynamic field was much stronger during the embryo's development. We also know that the metabolic process generally slows down in a steady progression from birth to old age. Our problem may well be that we view this process as inevitable. Scientists are more willing to believe that senility becomes a self-fulfilling prophecy when people "think old." Protection against senility essentially involves psychological protection against accepting well-defined roles for the aged perpetuated in an insensitive society.

According to the American Psychiatric Association (which certainly does a lot of its own unnecessary stigmatizing), senility involves impairment of the general intellectual process and emotional stability.

Studies show that the breakdown of a substance called amyloid, associated with immunoglobulin, an infection-fighting protein, may also quickly speed up the aging process. It is now being suggested, however cautiously, that amyloid may be instrumental in nerve-cell deterioration in the brain. One thing seems to be clear, however: amyloid accumulates in people in varying amounts. Can mental processes lower the immune system here too?

89

The work of Wilhelm Reich, a German-born psychoanalyst, has been a vital part of the great controversy concerning "life energies." In today's new context of bio-energy, his extensive theory and research are being revived. Reich believed that a life energy he called orgone existed everywhere in varying degrees. Like Reichenbach's Od, it penetrates everything at different speeds. Life, for Reich, meant that an organism was an organized part of the huge orgone ocean and that it metabolized this life energy according to its species' potential. In his experiments, Reich postulated the bions, "microscopically visible vesicles of functioning energy and transitional forms from non-living to living matter." The bion, according to Reich, is "the elementary functional unit of all living matter. It carries a specific amount of orgone energy which makes it function in a specific way biologically."

To demonstrate the existence of orgone, Reich invented an accumulator which, he claimed, captured and concentrated orgone. The outside of this box was organic and the inside metallic. He reasoned:

> *Since the former absorbs the energy while the latter reflects it, there is an accumulation of energy. The organic covering takes up the energy from the atmosphere and transmits it to the metal on the inside. The metal radiates the energy to the outside, into the organic material and to the inside into the space of the accumulator. The movement of energy towards the inside is free while toward the outside it is being stopped.*

In 1956, however, Reich was arrested. The United States Food and Drug Administration had earlier won a court injunction against the use of the accumulator. At the time, Reich believed that cancer patients could be helped by it, if not cured. He had violated the injunction, but did not hire a lawyer to defend him in court, believing that the court had no jurisdiction over scientific investigation. Reich was sentenced to two years, but died on November 3, 1957, in Lewisburg Penitentiary, after serving less than a year.

In light of recent data on the relationship between mind and body in the activation or prevention of disease, Reich's views on cancer are extremely significant. He believed that blockages of the natural flow of orgone were largely responsible for the onset of cancer. Therapy for Reich meant dealing with any mental or physical disposition which could create what he called armoring. He believed that this energy flow was disrupted as cells receive an extra amount of energy which may be trapped by repressed anxieties and other mental attitudes. As this surplus increases, the cell builds up to an explosion point. He believed that radiation therapy could be harmful because it could enable the explosion point to speed up. Psychologist Bruno Klopfer has added that in order to repress their emotions, many people use up large portions of their life energies, thus making them more susceptible to cancer.

While recent work by Robert Becker and others adds to our knowledge of the electric or biomagnetic nature of life and suggests that future healing therapies will involve the use of artificial fields to correct energy distribution in the body, the psychoanalytic flavor in Reich's work also suggests that this will not be enough. If a person's mental activity is unchecked and it is not seen as part of the unique way each person processes information, then any effect can at best be temporary, for it will not deal with the total information matrix of which each of us is a vital part.

Part Three

Chapter Seven

The
Great
Debate

"Maybe all the magicians will pull rabbits out of hats and saw women in half," whispered Jan Merta, who was seated beside me at the large conference table. For someone who had been accused of deception, he was being exceptionally congenial. A Montreal newspaper columnist had interviewed him when she learned he was to teach an introductory class on psychic phenomena at the downtown branch of the YMCA. The interview allowed Jan to express his belief that psychic research was achieving greater scientific respectability and to drum up publicity for the course.

Its publication, however, had angered a local magician. His subsequent rebuttal in the same newspaper claimed that all that passed as psychic phenomena was total bunk, and that people like Jan were exploiting a gullible public.

During the interview with Jan, the columnist had been irritated by one of his favorite demonstrations. "Until he placed a lighted cigarette on his tongue," she wrote, "I couldn't make up my mind what he was—dilettante or on-the-level student in a worthwhile field." The magician, who had never met Jan, added that the demonstration was "an outright lie, a stunt, nothing more," and claimed he had an entire file of cigarette tricks alone.

These charged remarks had set the stage for a public debate. I was invited to help Jan state his case and to balance the strong alliance between columnist and magician. I didn't approve of Jan's willingness to demonstrate anything which implied a psychic talent, but having discussed the nature of psychic phenomena with him several times, I understood his cigarette demonstration in

95

a context that both magician and columnist were not prepared nor willing to consider.

The magician was first to speak. Staring nervously at the large crowd, he slowly walked to the microphone and beamed a smile. "I come here on a serious matter which doesn't have to become too serious," he began. "I am attacking the entire phony field of occultism, and I am challenging Jan Merta in particular for several statements he made." In rhetorical style, he first emotionally condemned psychic researchers for leaving themselves open to grand deception, questioned the kinds of statistical techniques that were being used and then turned his attention to Jan. Waving a copy of the article on Jan published in *New Horizons,* he emphasized that the person who held the dowsing rod and who battled Jan's mental command had chosen to call himself T-53 rather than provide his correct name.

Sensing that he was winning over the audience, the magician also derided what he called the wish-fulfillment of all those who claimed they saw glowing energy around the dowsing rod. What had been advertised as a serious debate was quickly degenerating into a Sunday afternoon of ridicule and character assassination.

"I never claimed I was a psychic," said Jan when his turn came to speak. "A demonstration is a way to test some of my theoretical assumptions." There was a touch of frustration and resignation in his voice, but I knew he was motivated to at least defend himself against the claim that his cigarette demonstration was nothing but a cheap trick.

When Jan was a psychology student at McGill University, he became interested in the phenomenon of firewalking and wondered how a firewalker could protect himself against serious injury. Masahiko Muramatsu, the chief of plastic surgery at Koto Hospital in Tokyo, has explained that even a split-second contact with heat over 140 degrees Fahrenheit is enough for protein in the walker's foot to begin breaking down and become transformed into a pure energy state. Furthermore, exposure to a temperature of at least 167 degrees Fahrenheit will cause the skin to blister within one second. The age-old question had intrigued Jan: Was there a trick to fire immunity or a valid psychophysiological explanation which could be tested?

Two psychic investigators have offered very similar explanations for fire immunity. Mayne Coe, Jr. has theorized that moisture secreted by sweat glands forms tiny globules on the skin's surface and that this layer protects a person from heat penetration. In *Beyond Telepathy*, Andrija Puharich, a well-known medical scientist and inventor, wrote that "the tongue and other mucous membrane surfaces of the body are ... covered with moisture and this secretion is principally regulated by the cholinergic system." Cholinergia can be defined as a state of relaxation and well-being characterized by the activation of the parasympathetic nervous system. According to Puharich, a person in this state could secrete adequate moisture to protect the skin from intense heat.

After studying these two theories and believing they were sound, Jan decided he would personally test his convictions. At a blacksmith's shop in Montreal, with a camera recording every movement, he repeatedly placed his hands and tongue in contact for short periods of time with a metal bar heated up to 2642 degrees Fahrenheit.

He therefore concluded that a technique of maintaining a steady and relaxed state of mind could to some extent explain why some groups of deeply religious people are able to walk over hot coals without injury. Invariably such people believe they are protected by a divine force. Preparation for fire-walking often involves prayer, sexual abstinence, special diet and other rigorous measures over a lengthy period. Every year, for example, at A Shingon temple near Kyoto, Buddhists walk across burning embers. Their stride, accompanied by chanting, is steady, their gaze is hypnotic and they appear oblivious to any outside stimulation. Variations of this ritual have also served as truth-finding trials in a number of societies. In Central Tanzania, East Africa, for example, a Tagoru suspected of lying must vindicate himself by reaching into a pot of boiling water or sheep's fat and retrieve a stone without experiencing pain or injury. "If I am lying," he says aloud, "the test will harm me; if I am speaking the truth, nothing will happen."

The idea that body and consciousness are branches of the same tree sheds further light on this process. Recently at the Menninger Foundation's Voluntary Controls Project, Elmer Green tested Jack Swartz, who is widely known for his ability to control his bodily functions. Burning ash was held against his skin for as long as ten seconds, but careful monitoring of Swartz's physiological condition indicated that he was experiencing very little stress before, during, and after this experience. This obviously challenges well-reinforced causal modes of thinking. Clearly an "impossible" behavior such as fire-walking, which continues to be a ritual handed down through generations in Greece, Algeria, Ceylon, India, Malaysia, Bali, Fiji, and Japan must be examined in cultural contexts very different from our own. In *The Crack in the Cosmic Egg*, Joseph Chilton Pearce has explained precisely what state of mind seems to be required:

> ...*The cause-effect of fire burn underlies the physical world.... But fire does not have to burn a person in this particular case at this particular time. Neither does cancer have to kill this particular person at this particular time; nor do any of the other grim dragons of necessity have to apply to this person or that person, nor to any person who can believe in another way, or another construct.*
>
> *Is there a pattern? Yes. There is the conscious desire for the experience, the asking of the question. There is the detachment from the commonplace; the commitment to replace*

the conventional with a new construct; the
passion and decorum—the intensive prepara-
tion, the gathering of materials for the answer;
the freedom to be dominated by the subject
of desire—the sudden seizure, the break-
through of mind that gives the inexplicable
convictions that it can, after all, be done; and
then the serving of the new construct, the
instant application.

This process can also be described in terms of an information-processing model. The evolving self can be seen as
testing one probable reality after another. Certain reality
constructs become more dominant than others. The firewalker who has accepted certain basic tenets of his culture may create the strong reality that fire does *not* burn.
In this sense, Jan's deep conviction that both Coe and
Puharich offered a valid explanation which enabled him to
create the correct state of mind and to emerge unscathed
in his own experiment. He therefore involved himself
"psychically" in the control of his own mind and body.
Unfortunately, Jan's cigarette demonstration for the
columnist was too superficial a way of describing what he
was capable of achieving. It was naïve to assume that she
would make a great effort to understand an unusual
phenomenon in the total context of his extending his
sensory awareness.

During his talk at the YMCA, however, Jan did express
himself clearly and in great detail. But even this did not
evoke any honest attempt to understand his experiences.
The magician was not interested in autobiography, he
wanted action. The columnist appeared equally eager for
a demonstration. They both wanted to test him.

When Jan completed his fire-walking explanation, the
columnist immediately challenged him. "In an earlier
interview, you claimed to not only be a researcher but to
have psychic powers. Is that right? Will you repeat the
experiment you did for me earlier with the lighted
cigarette on your tongue?" Jan was bewildered by this

sudden request. Hadn't the columnist listened to what he had tried so hard to explain?

"Wait a minute," the magician interrupted. "Will you do this demonstration on my terms? Will you allow me to wipe off your tongue before you do it?"

"Yes, I'll do it," said Jan with a forced smile. "Why not?" He then looked at me sheepishly as if to ask if I thought he was crazy, but he had already made up his mind. It was his way of showing that he was fearless and adaptable to any situation.

The magician quickly wiped Jan's tongue with a cloth, and Jan immediately put out the cigarette with one lick. Cameras clicked. The audience gasped and then roared with approval. Their Sunday had not been wasted after all. Only a few people sadly shook their heads and understood what had occurred.

Two weeks later, I met a popular Montreal radio personality who was also an amateur magician. He had seen the striking newspaper photos of Jan's tongue squelching the cigarette and was disgusted by the whole affair. "It's nothing but a cheap trick," he quipped. "I wouldn't have that guy on my show even if all the local talent moved to Spain."

With the growing public interest in psychic phenomena, many more magicians have surfaced to attack the "psychic conspiracy." I have no doubt that there have been many "debates." Recently, two magicians have even set up a foundation to "stop the psychic movement."

The main target in the "psychic" community thus far has been Israeli-born Uri Geller, who claims to have been able to bend the hands of his watch—with psychokinesis alone—at age seven. Geller subsequently became a stage success in Israel and came to the attention of Andrija Puharich. A group of metallurgists convinced Puharich that a needle Geller claimed to have broken by sheer concentration had not been tampered with. Puharich, who had been searching for gifted subjects, convinced Geller to come to the United States to be tested at the Stanford Research Institute, a large American think-tank well known for its military-oriented contract work.

Before his arrival, however, Puharich had already done some of his own preliminary testing with Geller. Here is a brief summary of tests he conducted between November 17, 1972 and April 14, 1973, which immediately attracted the attention of the psychic research community in the United States and Canada:

1. Breaking metal objects. Repeatability—98 out of 102.
2. Moving clock hands—51 out of 56.
3. Moving compass needles—25 out of 30.
4. Dematerialization of metal objects—15 out of 20.
5. Rematerialization of the same objects—12 out of 20.

Several months before the publication of *Uri*, Puharich was interviewed in *Psychic,* a major magazine devoted to psi phenomena:

> When I got to Israel I found out that there was some kind of intelligence behind Uri Geller but I couldn't pin it down. So I pushed Uri into giving me some proof of what's behind this whole business. He dematerialized the inside brass cartridge of a Parker pen that was locked in a wooden box. It was gone, disappeared. Two days later Uri said, "Andrija, I'm going to get the proof you want." After a drive in the suburbs of Tel Aviv to a field, I heard some cricket-like sounds. And there in the field is what people call a UFO—a disk-shaped, metal object with a blue light flashing on top. I said, "Ah, now I have some evidence." I had fast night film in a Super-8 movie camera and I started shooting. Uri said, "You can't go near it, but I have to go aboard." From fifty yards away I believed that I saw him entering this thing; I think, "Well, goodbye Uri, I'll never see you again." I keep shooting. Ten minutes later he appears, holding something. I look at it and it's my

> *brass cartridge from the inside of my Parker pen with my markings on it, so I know it's mine ... So I said, "Oh, boy, now I've got a movie of a UFO, of you entering and now I've got this physical proof that something that disappeared two days ago came through. I've got a case." But then the cartridge in the Super-8 camera vanished, dematerialed in about ten minutes. There was my evidence. ...*

That story immediately resulted in growing bewilderment on the part of many of Puharich's colleagues, a few of whom suggested with a degree of seriousness that he be studied as well. Since the publication of *Uri*, in which Puharich weaves an extraordinary tale of extraterrestrial intelligences in a spaceship called Spectra repeatedly contacting him and Geller, (who apparently has been chosen as an ambassador to prepare mankind for an eventual landing), critics have had a wild time questioning Puharich's sanity. The book has been condemned as fraudulent, silly, and a tremendous shot in the arm for critics of more "respectable" paranormal research and theory. Many scientists who have recently granted parapsychological research increasing recognition have seen the kinds of episodes described in *Uri* as detrimental to the entire field.

This feeling is very understandable. Psychic researchers have been battling critics for many decades and parapsychology's history reveals a long, hard struggle for scientific recognition. William James, for example, one of the principal founders of the American Society for Psychical Research first became interested in a case which more or less inaugurated the battle on this continent. Mrs. Leonore Piper, a Bostonian, had attracted great attention due to her ability to provide extraordinary detail about deceased personalities. Cautious and skeptical at first about the medium's claims, James experienced firsthand evidence—like Puharich—and later wrote:

> *I am persuaded of the medium's honesty and of the genuiness of her trance; and*

> *although at first disposed to think that the hits she made were either coincidences, or the result of knowledge on her part of who the sitter was and of his or her family affairs, I now believe her to be in possession of a power as yet unexplained.*

In a now-famous retort to his critics, James wrote:

> *If you will let me use the language of the professional logicshop, a universal proposition can be made untrue by a particular instance. If you wish to upset the laws that all crows are black, you mustn't seek to show that no crows are: it is enough if you prove one single crow to be white. My own white crow is Mrs. Piper.*

How you go about proving one crow is white is another matter. The subsequent problems encountered by the Parapsychology Laboratory established at Duke University in 1934 under the directorship of William MacDougall and later headed by Joseph Rhine serves as an important reminder. Rhine introduced a testing procedure involving a deck of twenty-five cards with five different geometrical shapes on their faces. To investigate telepathy, for example, the subject in an experiment would try to guess what card an "agent" in another room was concentrating on. A score of more than five correct guesses in twenty-five attempts would be seen as evidence for telepathy. Rhine also used the term *psychokinesis* to describe direct mental action on matter. A subject, for example, would try to influence tossed dice to fall according to a pre-established total. Statistical interpretation of the results would be conducted in accordance with the laws of probability.

Critics were eager to question the experimental designs used in these experiments, what they felt was lack of self-criticism among psychic investigators, poor reporting and excessive claims, and of course, the inability of researchers to predict outcomes based on their previous findings. Rhine's ESP cards were criticized because

103

apparently it was *once* possible to see through them if they were held to the light in a certain way. High ESP scores by subjects were viewed as "runs of luck" because of the tendency for scores to drop when a subject was tested repeatedly. Other critics have simply rejected ESP because they could not understand it. Psychologist Donald Hebb once honestly remarked:

> *Why do we not accept ESP as psychological fact? Rhine has offered enough evidence to convince us on almost any other issue where one could make some guess as to the mechanism of the disputed process. Personally, I do not accept ESP for a moment because it does not make any sense. I cannot see what other base my colleagues have for rejecting it, but my own rejection of Rhine's view, is, in the literal sense, prejudiced.*

What remains a major issue in experimental procedure, of course, is the tremendous faith many researchers have in their own criteria of validity. It is indisputable that biases and personal self-interests serve to determine many of these criteria. (But this is true in all scientific work.) The controversial case of the famous medium Eusapia Palladino who lived at the turn of this century provides an acute example which surely has its modern equivalents. She often bluntly admitted that she would prefer to levitate a table by cheating, since using her real psychic powers was very tiring. Therefore, the conflicting reports on her talents were all open to question. Poor controls and overreliance on some investigators' credentials marred the entire drama which spanned almost three decades. Similarly, the late Arthur Ford, another renowned medium, has recently been exposed as having often used deceit. Given access to Ford's letters, diaries, and scrapbooks, Allan Spraggett and William Rauscher found that he had done exhaustive research on many of his clients and had amassed thousands of obituaries from all over the United States. Was Ford at all genuine?

Spraggett and Rauscher believe so, but the controversy is only beginning.

The central point about the Palladino and Ford dramas as well as the ongoing controversy over Uri Geller, and the validity of all psi research is that scientific "credentials" play a large role in determining the credibility of an event or phenomenon. Likewise, scientific selectivity of what events are worth studying and subsequent public dramatizing in the form of publicity and colleague endorsement have a great deal to say about the nature of scientific progress. Puharich, for example, has always been viewed as a maverick in the psychic field. Compared with many of his more conservative colleagues who spend much of their lives repeating the same experiments over and over again in the hope that "truly scientific" measures will be obtained, he is no doubt often seen as a nuisance. He ingeniously attracts attention to theoretical assumptions about man and universe that do not easily lend themselves to more standard experimental work. He is therefore expendable.

It has not been unusual at all that many parapsychologists have not attempted to place Puharich's remarks about extraterrestrial intelligence in some theoretical perspective. But, anyone reasonably familiar with the psychic field knows that claims for Uri Geller's abilities are by no means unique. A carefully contrived publicity jaunt and some scientific endorsement has unfortunately given many critics and the public the impression that Geller alone has the potential to revolutionize science as well as completely invalidate psychic phenomena if he is found to be fraudulent. This is an ominous and a completely unnecessary attitude to which Puharich himself in his enthusiasm over Geller has contributed. Those familiar with so-called "miracles" performed in other cultures should know better. For example, in *Autobiography of a Yogi,* Paramahansa Yogananda, founder of the Self-Realization Fellowship in America, has written of the guru who was the founder of his faith: "In turn with

105

the infinite all-encompassing Will, Babaji is able to command the elementary atoms to combine and manifest themselves into any form. . . . Babaji created this beautiful mansion out of his mind and is holding its atoms together by the power of his will, even as God's thoughts created the earth and His will maintains it." Are we to simply write off this belief as well or are we willing to "locate" a theoretical and cultural context that will accommodate it?

Having been trained in the scientific tradition and reared in accordance with the doctrine of cause and effect, I have found it extremely difficult to experience the world in any other way. Unfortunately, scientific procedure becomes reified and becomes an end in itself. In the guise for "truth," human possibilities in light of this system of "knowing" the world are ordered according to a hierarchy of what is deemed more probable. Someone like Uri Geller gets singled out primarily because many scientists resist exploring the possible connections between what Geller may be capable of and the vast amount of "unexplained" phenomena in everyday life.

I believe that one of the main reasons for this is the deep-seated tendency in current parapsychological research to "prove" that there are worlds beyond the so-called normal senses which can be tapped. I suspect much of the hostility toward claims of psychic ability is grounded in this attitude: People fear behavior or events described as outside the boundaries of what is "normal." Ironically, what gets in the way of more imaginative theory and research as well as a less emotional attitude toward the "unexplained" *is the reliance on intellectual foundations which foster the illusion that a state of normality exists.* This paradigm or "base line" gives rise to an imaginary line between what is normal and paranormal, "psychic" or not "psychic."

Therefore, something as extraordinary as Puharich's claims or the claims of someone "seeing" a UFO in the state of Mississippi does not fit into the step by step attempt to explain the unusual in terms of what is considered acceptable or "typical" human behavior. Our Western heritage has well-reinforced the need to see the unusual from well-defined standards of what is acceptable. The entire thrust of science and its periodic revolutions testifies to this fact. Paradigms govern research and theory and ignore certain categories of information. What bothers me the most about the current obsession with making parapsychology respectable is that in the process, numerous human beliefs are designated as untenable, partly in the hope that the "extremes" of human experience will not get in the way of "serious" work. This is especially maddening when modern psychic research does not even have any theoretical standards upon which such distinctions can be made. Little wonder that critics have had such an influential impact on public and professional sentiment. Furthermore, the current psychic sensationalism emerging hand-in-hand with the scientific work can be directly attributed to this "imaginary line syndrome." People want to cross the line into "psychism" quickly instead of understanding that there is a continuity to human expression. Clearly, a much greater awareness of social dynamics needs to be injected into this entire complex movement. A greater awareness of how definitions of human behavior are processed in evolving political and cultural contexts is imperative especially at a time when more people are taking psychic phenomena more seriously.

Whenever I'm asked if I believe in psychic phenomena or if I'm psychic, I try to gauge the person's expectations before I respond. Often I sigh deeply and simply say that we shouldn't close our minds to anything which lacks satisfactory explanation. The fact is that I believe what we usually call "psychic" *in principle is no different from what we call "normal" or ordinary behavior.*

At a time when more and more people appear to *want* recognition for their psychic or "extrasensory" talents, this is an unpopular position. I am suggesting that those

107

who wish to make others more aware of psychic potential have made a great tactical error in creating and reifying distinctions between one type of behavior and another. We have been too unwilling to examine in a comprehensive way how behavior is generated—and accepted as more "real" than other behavior—in a continually evolving society. We have been reluctant to probe how human beings process environmental information on a mass level and how certain aspects of this behavior are characterized in different ways. If scientific classification is an inevitable reflection of deep-seated reality constructs culturally activated and reinforced, perhaps we are fearful of really opening up our reality in conceptual terms and to recognize the fragile quality of our most cherished beliefs and scientific concepts.

Thus far, in this book, I have been attempting to emphasize the continuity of human behavior. In a very *preliminary* way I am presenting the idea that the universe is an evolving informational matrix in continuous and dynamic states of organization and that information exchange occurs amongst these continuous states according to not static but evolving universal laws.

Man is seen as an evolving informational state, holographic in nature. This suggests that the continuous state of organizing information called man incorporates *all* the information of the universal matrix of which it is a dynamic part. What we call human birth may be seen as a particular informational exchange among all states, reflecting a unique organizational state of the universal matrix.

Another way of stating this is that *a human being is a unique blueprint of an exact moment of universal evolution.* Each human blueprint, then, uniquely incorporates the state of this particular universal matrix and in turn simultaneously contributes to all other exchanges. You and I therefore each possess a *unique* quality of the whole, while incorporating all universal information.

This quality or behavioral disposition is affected

continuously by the nature of information exchange occurring everywhere in the universe and is a continuous and evolving process. What we call life, then can be seen as the maintenance and evolution of certain informational states. What we call death is the final transmutation of these states. According to this model of information processing, time is the evolving configuration or current of this universal matrix. Each information exchange contributes to the rate and flow of time. A human being, an evolving informational blueprint, will therefore experience time uniquely, in terms of his own patterns of life maintenance and evolution.

What, then, is a society? It too can be seen as an evolving informational state, holographic in nature and maintained by patterns of information exchange. What we call political, philosophical, and cultural institutions as well as organized systems of knowledge (science included) are also continuous and evolving states of information. Visible human behavior, according to this model can be viewed simply as physically manifested information exchange at any given moment.

What is dominant in a society, as we explored earlier in this book, is therefore an illusory and extremely fragile phenomenon. The "self," as well as a society, can be seen as multidimensional because of its ongoing information processing. What appears as dominant information to an individual is due to a unique evolving relationship to the universal matrix.

Numerous studies in what we have called *sensory* deprivation, which isolate people in sound- and lightproof rooms, show that once a well-reinforced thinking process which dominates in everyday life stops, the mind is overwhelmed by a flood of nonordinary imagery. In one study conducted at McGill University in Montreal by psychologist Donald Hebb, student volunteers experienced what we call childish emotional response and hallucinations after twenty-four hours. A somewhat amusing but instructive experience of a night spent in the king's chamber of the Great Cheops Pyramid is described by Paul Brunton. Finding himself completely locked away within the huge walls, Brunton "tuned in" to the world inside:

> Shadows began to flit to and fro through the shadowless room; gradually these took more definite shape and malevolent countenances appeared suddenly quite close to my own face. Sinister images rose plainly before my mind's eye. Then a dark apparition advanced, looked at me with fixed sinister regard and raised its hands in a gesture of menace, as though seeking to inspire me with awe. Age-old spirits seemed to have crept out of the neighboring necropolis, a necropolis so old that the mummies had crumbled away inside their stone sarcophagi; the shades that clung to them made their unwelcome ascent to the place of my vigil. . . .

I suppose Brunton could be accused of eloquently exaggerating his experience, but from what we know about the sharp reduction of routinized sensory input and its effect on the mind's ability to coherently maintain a state of focused awareness, what he saw can be likened to the kinds of images people receive when in solitary confinement, stranded on a desert, or when simply bored. John Lilly, known for his innovative work with dolphins and his experimentation with hallucinogens, well documented in *The Center of the Cyclone*, has been recently involved in a series of "deprivation" studies involving an isolation tank. "In the tank," he has stated, "we are up against a world where the usual cues don't work; so we are confronted with our evasions, our fears. . . . Once you can get into the tank with no preprogramming and no expectations, you are able to experience new and novel phenomena."

These examples indicate what occurs when one's customary and conscious information processing and decision making based on well-reinforced cues is suddenly

110

altered. The solid world of customary appearances dissolves into a fragile and quickly changing sensory stream of consciousness. No longer do we have our "two feet on solid ground," but our minds become part of an informational pool where surfacing images unpredictably assault our patterns of informational organization.

What I'm offering here is the recognition that all categorization of human behavior as normal, psychic or whatever, is itself a result of continuous information processing. The fact that we may be able to learn to be more "psychic" is simply a way of saying that we can alter our patterns of information processing. One reason why this cannot be a simple overnight process is that we, in effect, are *blueprints* which can evolve, and which can activate any information available in the universal matrix. However, this requires a patterning of this information and an organization lest we dissolve into a chaotic whirlpool of imagery.

Applying the information-processing model to a variety of human experiences, we can view human behavior in more comprehensive terms; remove some of the sensationalistic and denigrating attributes we have bestowed upon genuine human beliefs; and celebrate the human potential that we are capable of greatly developing.

Chapter Eight

Examples
of
Information
Processing

I. EXTRATERRESTRIALS

With the discovery that many of the building block molecules of life can be found in the vastness of space, scientists have become more confident that life exists on planets of other suns. Just fifty years ago, even the existence of planets outside the solar system was viewed skeptically. It is now increasingly believed that communication between other planetary intelligences may occur via the electromagnetic spectrum and that it may be possible to intercept and decode it. Cornell astronomer Carl Sagan, author of *The Cosmic Connection,* has written:

> *We may be very much like the inhabitants of an isolated valley in New Guinea who communicate with villages in the next valley by drum and runner but have no idea that there is a vast international radio traffic going on around them, over them and through them.*

Duncan Lunan, an amateur astronomer and president of the Scottish Association for Technology and Research in Astronautics, claims he decoded a series of radio "echoes" which were first detected by French, Dutch and Norwegian radio researchers during the 1920's. He believes that these irregular signals come from a space

113

probe providing us with a map of an advanced civilization's home base. His graph reveals that the dots appear to represent the constellation Boötes and point to a star called Epsilon Boötes 103 light-years away.

Lunan's critics have attempted to discredit this discovery arguing that he is jumping to conclusions. Others view the odds against Lunan's findings as being merely fantastic coincidence, and Kenneth Gatland, vice-president of the British Inter-Planetary Society, has suggested that "the messages could have started being beamed to Earth thousands of years ago and have since been waiting for us to gain sufficient scientific knowledge to interpret them."

Lunan's discovery only adds to the growing controversy and the interest in the idea that extraterrestrial intelligences have been trying to contact us, or in fact have already visited us. In *Chariots of the Gods?* Erich von Däniken asks us to consider that our entire culture is a conspiracy of sorts. His thesis is that extraterrestrials visited our planet and paninsemination of our species has taken place. Von Däniken's numerous books point to planetary enigmas such as mysterious airfields, cave drawings, as well as art objects found across the planet depicting figures wearing what look like space helmets. While von Däniken's research has recently been severely challenged, in part as a deliberate fabrication as well as being based on selective omission of a wide range of data, he nevertheless has stimulated a great interest in these enigmas and has perhaps made us more willing to consider, as William James once wrote, that "actualities seem to float in a wider sea of possibilities out of which they were chosen."

A look at some recent thinking in physics reflects such a growing willingness on numerous fronts. One view undergoing strong critical scrutiny is that an expanding universe was generated by an extraordinary explosion of dense primordial matter resulting in the evolution of stars, galaxies and other celestial objects. This view, called the "big bang theory," it appears, is much too incomplete. We have high-energy physics to blame. Paul Dirac won the 1933 Nobel Prize in physics for his prediction on mathematical grounds that antimatter should exist. In 1932 the positron, having the exact mass of its opposite, the electron, was detected. Then came the antiproton, further revealing the symmetry between particles and antiparticles. Could this also mean that the universe has equal quantities of matter and antimatter?

Oskar Klein, a Swedish physicist, believes it does but suggests that if the primordial explosive matter as described in the "big bang theory" had contained antimatter as well, the original nucleus would have been destroyed. Klein has therefore postulated that the universe originally had been comprised of a vast, dilute gaseous cloud, or in more technical terms, a plasma of electrifying particles which slowly contracted as a result of gravitation. The cloud's radius eventually shrunk to a point where the widely dispersed particles of matter and antimatter began to increasingly collide, thus producing sufficient quantities of radiation pressure to overcome gravitational attraction. The cloud with its condensed galaxies then began to expand and today represents the astronomer's expanding universe.

The question which naturally arises is whether antiworlds exist, even within our own galaxy. Geoffrey Burbridge and Fred Hoyle, for example, believe that matter and antimatter worlds meet in the huge Crab constellation and their collision may be responsible for electromagnetic waves being emitted equal to the intensity of 100 billion Hiroshima-like atom bombs per second.

Klein has also described our universe as a possible metagalaxy, only one of many such galactic assemblages. In this respect, some fascinating information comes our way from scientists who are studying the life cycle of stars. Hydrogen atoms cluster in space due to gravitational attraction. Increasing densities and pressure

115

eventually generate thermonuclear burning and the life of a star begins. The cycle ends when gravitation has necessitated the dead star's complete collapse into a black hole. John Wheeler, a Princeton physicist, believes that this event could be a signal for the eventual gravitational collapse of our universe.

Where does the matter inside these black holes go? To another universe? Physicist Robert M. Hjellming of the National Radio Observatory at Greenbank, West Virginia, has speculated that the passage of matter from a black hole would emerge in another universe through a connecting antithetical white hole. And Wheeler has even suggested that there must be a superspace possessing many or perhaps an infinite number of multidimensional universes.

The implication is that there exist great chains of parallel worlds in other dimensions of reality. Oxford nuclear physicist D. H. Wilkinson, noting that subatomic particles such as the neutrino hardly interact with matter as they penetrate through the earth, has written:

> Perhaps there do exist universes interpenetrating with ours; perhaps of a high complexity perhaps containing their own forms of awareness; constructed out of other particles and other intereactions than those which we now know, but awaiting discovery through some common but elusive interaction we have yet to spot. . .

In light of these remarks, the hope that radio astronomers have in communicating with extraterrestrials may be based on too narrow a scientific view. The millions of dollars now being spent to develop better and better communications equipment is a good example of how scientists tend to filter out important exploration. In fact, there is an unwarranted arrogance about seeing communication with extraterrestrials in purely "out there" terms. Carl Sagan, apparently, is such a champion. On the Dick Cavett television show, he made an attempt to poke fun at a man who claimed he was kidnapped by extraterrestrials. Sagan's reasoning, which completely dismissed the man's story, was based on the idea that "it's tough to travel between the stars because the stars are extremely far apart."

In a very basic way, Sagan's reasoning completely evades the question of how we may be related to the universal matrix. In terms of the information-processing model, we are just as much "extraterrestrial" as we are human beings," but in different states of energy transmutation and existing on different planes of organizing reality. *We are the UFO's:*

There is no absolute line separating evolving universal states. Outward appearances of categories and clear demarcations are completely illusory. Scientists such as Carl Sagan operate from paradigmatic ground rules, unwisely viewing their own states of consciousness as separate from the vast biological web of energy buildup and breakdown and thus they can feel confident that from their "solid" viewpoints, certain forms of communication are impossible.

I would argue that someone who claims to be kidnapped by extraterrestrials is exhibiting behavior no different in principal from the behavior we deem appropriate and normal but merely behavior which our more dominant focused states of awareness refuse to activate as equally real. Depending on the nature of the informational organizing state of the society, this behavior will be accorded different chances of being seen as real. The present state of societal evolution and information processing apparently cannot as yet activate such experiences as dominant patterns. Why some people and not others can activate these kinds of realities may be due to their unique blueprint activity.

II. "FORTEANA"

A library easily could be completely devoted to strange sightings. The most comprehensive

117

surely was Charles Fort's, whose shoeboxes of newspapers and periodical clippings have become legendary. Fort had details of snowflakes as large as saucers, blue moons, rains of frogs, red rains, mud rains, and almost anything you can imagine in his "sanatorium of overworked coincidences," a filing system of over twenty-five thousand notes. He believed that nothing could be isolated and attacked science for its obsession with its procedure of isolating events. In typical Fortean fashion, he wrote: "In some so-called savage tribes the feeble-minded are held in great respect." Over the years, however, many of the strange sightings recorded by Fort have been "explained away" by scientists as natural phenomena. But what isn't? There are some events which are scientifically explained and others which are not. This should have no bearing on the validity of their reality. Fort was arguing that scientists simply overlooked natural phenomena that they didn't want to understand or that they claimed were impossible. Science patterns what it wishes to investigate and isolates its target population.

John Keel, author of *Strange Creatures from Time and Space* once wrote that this selectivity goes on in psychic research, as well as among groups competing for the "more real" quality of their strange sightings:

> *Whenever we fail to uncover solid evidence to support our observations of paranormal phenomena, we tend to indulge in fanciful speculation. After chasing flying saucers for twenty-five years, we find we have no more real evidence than when we began, so we decide arbitrarily that they are spaceships from beyond our solar system. Since humming, buzzing multicolored UFO's hang around the lakes and rivers inhabited by plesiosaurs and their relatives, and the swamps and woodlands are frequented by Snallygasters, it should be obvious that all these things share a common cause.*
> *No one seriously contends that sea serpents*

are visitors from some other planet. Rather, it is becoming increasingly evident that all unexplained phenomena are connected in some inexplicable fashion. . . .

The reality of these things is not only unproved and unprovable, but the integration and logical, objective study of all these matters has been made impossible by the intrusion of belief. Loch Ness investigators sneer at the whole subject of UFO's; ufologists ignore Snallygaster reports; psychical researchers are so busy hunting ghosts that they have little time for flying saucers and monsters . . . although all these subjects produce the same effects.

From the standpoint of information-processing, *everything* can be considered to be a "strange phenomenon" until it is activated as *real.* If you ever saw something "strange" like the Bigfoot creature, it might take all your emotional and intellectual resources to convince yourself that it was real. But if you saw it, it *would* be real. In essence, "strange sightings" are basically those behaviors which have not been adequately activated as dominant and stable in our planetary consciousness, but this does not mean they do not and have not existed for a large number of people.

III. APPARITIONS, HAUNTINGS, AND VOICE PHENOMENA

Many people claim they have seen a ghost. The psychic literature is overflowing with stories of apparitions that appear suddenly during times of crises, after someone's death or simply at any time. An attempt to investigate this phenomenon has been a major interest in psychic research. One early view by Edmund Gurney was that apparitions were subjective, telepathically induced when an individual picked up a cue of some kind. Gurney later modified this view to accommodate collective visualizations arguing that "telepathic contagion" accounted for the phenomenon.

How then, do very large groups of people all see an apparition at the same time, and why do animals appear to detect them? A number of investigators have offered a variety of "field" explanations, arguing either that a fourth-dimensional field could explain this phenomenon or that apparitions were "soul bodies" who appeared to have a life of their own and were capable of responding to environmental conditions.

Recently, however, a number of psychic researchers have been paying closer attention to developments in the field of optics, and in particular to holography. This is basically a technique which photographically captures the reflected lightwaves of an object rather than the object's image. A laser beam, a coherent light, is then used to in effect "straighten out" the three-dimensional maze of circles and specks.

Barry Taff, a research associate at the Neuropsychiatric Institute at UCLA, in a recent article, pointed to the fascinating similarity between the properties of the hologram and what neurophysiologists know about memory. Any part of the hologram, for example, can reproduce the entire image until the part is so small that the image becomes blurred. If any part of the brain becomes damaged, memory is very often still totally functional. Taff reasons that "perhaps during the process of remembering, we are recreating the initial spatio-temporal frequency carrier on which the events are carried, which would allow the image and accompanying information to be recovered and recognized." The focusing mind, Taff suggests, can be likened to the coherence of a laser beam. Can this be the way that apparitions are activated? Can the mind sometimes activate the reality expressed by the apparition powerfully enough so that others can also visualize the same phenomenon? From the standpoint of information processing, information exchange, which is a dynamic ongoing process throughout every moment of our life, can be seen as holographic in nature. All information is potentially accessible but must be activated by a specific state of mind.

What then is a haunting? It is usually referred to as an apparition which is seen recurrently over a long period in one specific place. Early theories, such as those of Eleanor Sidgwick's, focused on the ability of an individual to "read" the conditions (for example) of a particular house where someone had died violently. The impressions in such a house would therefore be very strong and lasting. A relatively similar explanation by H. H. Price was that a psychic ether was impregnated with strong impressions and could be "recalled" under the right conditions. According to Price, a haunting was "a kind of deferred telepathy resulting in a postdated telepathic phantasm." More recently, W. G. Roll modified Sidgwick's theory, suggesting that a psi field of a house may be "read."

The main problem with these views is that they are primarily focused on the ability of a sensitive human being to be capable of such a "reading." There is evidence, however, that often people who have witnessed hauntings are incapable of extending this "sensitivity" to "reading" other events. Once again, this emphasis on "psychic" ability takes our attention away from the unique behavioral capacities of each and every individual. According to the information processing model, someone who "reads" a "haunted" house is proceeding *uniquely* in activating patterns which exist in some organizational state, but are primarily invisible and therefore less dominant manifestations of a part of the matrix of organizing information. The same can be said for the observations of large groups of people.

Recently there has been a sudden explosion of interest on this continent in what is called voice phenomena. In 1959 a Swedish film producer, Frederich Jurgenson, heard strange voices on tape recordings which appeared to be sentences spoken by people who had died. Several

121

years later Jurgenson worked closely with Konstantin Raudive, the late Latvian psychologist, in an attempt to reproduce this phenomenon. Raudive concluded that the voices were coming from people who had died and touched off a fascinating controversy. Hans Bender, a German parapsychologist, has countered that these voices are projected subconsciously by the experimenter. This has been vigorously disputed by a number of researchers, primarily because it is generally felt that subconscious symbology could not be transformed into verbal communications onto the magnetic tape.

In some ways, these phenomena can be seen as similar to apparition detection. Voices in most cases are very difficult to make out and usually require a highly trained ear. The fact that all information is continually capable of being activated and that it is being exchanged in numerous ways unknown to us, at the conscious level, should not be discounted. This, however, does not necessarily mean that specific entities known to those present are communicating the information in a direct and deliberate fashion. Instead, the phenomenon can be seen as simply another informational exchange process; not from an "out-there" reality but from an organic and dynamic process highly relevant to the experimenter.

IV. THE ETHERIC DOUBLE, THE ASTRAL BODY AND OUT-OF-BODY EXPERIENCES

If the material human body is essentially a by-product of an *organizing state* which has become relatively stable, the "etheric double," the theosophists' prephysical body of the bioplasmic body emphasized by work in Kirlian photography, may represent a more evolved segment of an organizing state's multidimensional energy continuum history. While it may be viewed as an almost exact duplicate preceding the physical bodily form, it can therefore also be defined as a more successful example of the many possible probable realities along this continuum capable of becoming manifested as dense physical bodies. Well-focused information processing can prevent other probable realities from becoming more dominant and drastically altering the individual's physically dominant organizing state. In this fashion, the physical body maintains its cooperative imagery but remains capable of both gradual or sudden changes.

What then is astral projection? This phenomenon of astral projection has been widely reported and appears to be common in most cultures. In the Fiji Islands, for example, awakening a sleeping person is considered dangerous. It is believed that the soul is wandering and may have difficulty returning to the physical body. In the West Indies, astral projection is known as hagging and it is believed that the hag who ritualistically sings a number of charm songs leaves the body in an unconscious state, takes on numerous appearances. Ancient Indian writings as well, refer to astral projections as "flying in the sky."

One of the oldest investigations of astral projection was published in 1883 in France by Adolphe D'Assier, who believed that astral activity occurred particularly during very deep sleep and coma. D'Assier wrote that the astral body never completely loses its relationship with the body, but is united with it by "an invisible plexus of invisible capillaries." This connection, often referred to as "the silver cord," appears throughout psychic literature.

Many of the investigations of astral projection have attempted to show that this occurrence is not purely imaginery but of an objective, semiphysical nature. In studying Ingo Swann, who in experimental conditions is asked to project himself to a vantage point in a room from which he can see objects in trays, Karlis Osis, Research Director of The American Society for Psychical Research, has shown that Swann's body while undergoing the astral experience maintains a normal range of heart rate, breathing, pulse, and blood pressure. Only brainwave

123

activity reveals a reduction. This is seen as a decrease in electrical activity. Swann has stated that he has been "very aware of the linear displacement of space and time," and that he has been "aware of other beings around who are not inhabiting bodies," but he doesn't "think of them in terms of ghosts or people who have gone to higher elevations or anything like that. Most of them have seemed to be in a very problematic state concerning their own existence. They seem to be very tortured individuals." We can speculate here that Swann may be "reading" organizing states which in the terms of his own unique way of processing information may be deflecting a number of emotional states,

Robert A. Monroe, author of *Journeys Out of the Body*, who began having out-of-body experiences unexpectedly, once pinched a person during one of his "trips" and left a mark on the person's skin. This perhaps can be viewed as a kind of psychokinetic action produced by a strong vitality similar to the kind of behavior of which some mediums are capable. For example, Eusapia Palladino, a very powerful physical medium, had a great need to rid herself of a strongly accumulated psychic energy. Her ability to produce rapping and levitation may have been a direct result of releasing the energy charged up in her etheric double.

In the case of the renowned physical medium, D. Dunglas Home, many knocks and raps were heard, particularly when he became ill. Where physical phenomena followed death, this is usually due to death coming very suddenly. In such cases, the double may have been supercharged, capable of maintaining itself in a more stable organizing state after life ceased in the physical body. Perhaps physical effects during out-of-body experiences are examples of an individual's relatively stable ability to activate another dimensional self. It is noteworthy that Edgar Cayce once had an astral projection during which he saw waxen images of people and was told in trance that these were shells left behind by

124

advancing souls. These shells had not yet disintegrated but remained at least minimally stable organizing states.

Probably the best survey of astral projection is by Robert Crookall. In *Mechanisms of Astral-Projection Denouement After Seventy Years,* Crookall accumulated a wide assortment of astral experiences and attempted to categorize the properties of astral bodies. For example, doubles of the living could or could not exhibit consciousness or initiative. Some doubles could exhibit certain physical properties and therefore were subjected to gravity, cast shadows, and could not pass through matter. Other doubles, Crookall pointed out, seemed to have no physical properties, could defy gravity and pass through walls. Some doubles could be seen and heard by almost everyone, others by only some. Still others were observed to leave the body as mist. Some doubles' movement was identical to that of the body, and others indicated a time lag.

Partially disembodied doubles of the dying in most cases seemed to operate similarly; however, a silver cord is not often seen. Completely disembodied doubles of the dead may move independently of the physical body. These categories that Crookall developed are largely based on the numerous testimonies and research conducted in the psychic field. Crookall may have unwittingly described the different properties of the organizing states of the multidimensional self, which having a life of their own, exist as probable selves and can be activated by an individual to provide new dimensions of universal information.

V. HEXING AND TELEPATHY

For six months, a small drawing of a sun bursting through clouds was pasted on my study window. My friend Matt advised me that this hex sign would bring about good weather. He had called while it was snowing and promptly tried to persuade me to go outdoors to tell the snow in a friendly manner that it should go away. Matt claims that he made rain clouds veer once, as well as having made the sun suddenly appear. He has been using hexes for several years for different purposes and is convinced that they work. Learning a little about the information-processing model, he was eager to see how I would view the work of a hex.

According to Lee Gandee, author of *Strange Experience: The Autobiography of a Hexenmeister,* "A Hex knows a thought to be a thing—a form with an electronic force-field—so when he arranges his motifs (hex signs) what he really is doing is sending out into the universe a telepathic blueprint image of what he wishes materialized." Throughout history there have been numerous imaginative methods of wishing for things. Every culture on this planet has had its own particular spells and hexes, thus reflecting the strong belief in universal forces which can be used for good or evil. Often these methods are used as part of impressive ceremonies designed to appeal to a god, demon, or cosmic force. For example, in *The Grimorium Verum,* a French magical textbook, there is an instruction for harming an enemy by driving a nail from an old coffin into his footprint. In any of the numerous European magical texts as well as ancient and secret manuscripts, there are many examples of prayers to be used to kill people or cause great pain. Often these prayers are to God asking for His help; it seems a person's motive is not very relevant! In *The Black Arts*, Richard Cavendish writes that "an exceptionally gifted and powerful magician may be able to kill by the sheer force of concentrated hatred, especially if his victim is someone of unusual sensitivity."

Clearly some symbolic link is used by the magician or Hex to establish a link between cause and effect. Here again, there are numerous methods. The link may be a magic word, prayer, secret formula or chant, a picture of a victim, and in the case of voodoo, a doll is sometimes

126

used. The person attempting to cause harm must attempt to sustain the force of hatred for as long as he can. The link used is a subconscious manifestation of conscious will. If a natural link is difficult to find, a charm can be used and placed, for example, in the victim's house. Often practitioners of black magic will simply mentally create a link charging it with their vital energy, allowing it to propel the energy to the victim. According to Gandee, "to be a witch one must be able to send sustained images far enough out to attract enough energy to effect the materialization. . . ." Gandee does not believe space is an obstacle. He explains that "experience" suggests that magic power is derived from the action of the mind at the subconscious level. A symbol is more potent than a naturalistic representation because a realistic drawing is interpreted mainly at the conscious level. In solitude and secrecy," he continues, "the mind thinks in symbols." Common universal symbols, for example, include a heart standing for love, an olive branch or dove for peace and a rabbit's foot for good fortune.

How this may "work" presents an opportunity to look more closely at information processing. Each individual, a by-product of universal energies and manifested as a relatively stable but organizing state as well as a creator of continuous probable realities, is an integral part of the universal matrix. Each individual, therefore, is both capable of drawing information from this matrix as well as directing information to it. This continuous broadcasting and receiving process is not uniform, and certainly only a very small part of all of it can be experienced at the conscious level. Each individual also is differently focused in consciousness. I suspect therefore, that when Matt desires sunshine, the hex sign he draws allows him to transfer energy from his focused state of consciousness into the universal matrix as a strong probable reality. The hex drawing, acting as a link, allows him to focus his broadcasting at another level of mind. Matt's success or failure, may have to do with his ability to "read" the

127

conditions which prevail which may allow a probable reality to become physically activated. This way, a specific kind of hex can be used.

Failure, I believe, is primarily indicative of not adequately "capturing" the current of universal information dynamics. A particular prayer, under the correct conditions, likewise may set in motion a reality which if produced with strong vitality can develop into a more stable organizing state. A prayer or a hex with a little energy will generate an organizing state that will lose more and more of its vitality unless it is somehow strongly reinforced. In the *The Seth Material* we learn that "the objective world is the end result of inner action." Seth explains that, "thoughts and images are formed into physical reality and become physical fact. They are propelled chemically. A thought is energy. It begins to produce itself physically at the moment of its conception." Seth also says:

> *The physical environment is as much a part of you ... as your body. Your control over it is quite effective, for you create it as you create your fingertip. ...Objects are composed of the same pseudo-material that radiates outward from your own physical image, only the higher intensity mass is different. When it is built up enough, you recognize it as an object. At low intensity mass, it is not apparent to you.*

Victims of black magic and hexes, generally, may be incapable of resisting thought directed patterns and therefore allow them to overwhelm their own patterns of information processing. The following fascinating case reported by psychiatrist Ronald Wintrob involving a hex death in Baltimore provides a good example:

> *A midwife informed the mothers of three baby girls born in the Florida swamps that a spell had been placed upon their daughters, who would all die young: the first, before her sixteenth birthday, the second before her*

twenty-first birthday and the third before her twenty-third. Years passed. The third young woman was admitted to a hospital with apparent congestive heart failure. She was in a state of panic and was hyperventilating. On questioning at length by her physicians several days later she broke down and related the outcome of the hex. The first girl died in an auto accident during her fifteenth year; the second was at a nightclub celebrating the end of the hex on her twenty-first birthday, when a fight broke out and several shots were fired. The third girl died two years later before her twenty-third birthday, presumably of congestive heart failure. . . .

Many doctors, of course, believe that a hex is autosuggestion of the most powerful kind. The victim becomes completely obsessed with the hex's intent. According to the information-processing model, once an individual incorporates a thought form from another individual as a base from which to build further thought forms, if it is a hex intending the person to die, incorporation of this reality will be increasingly activated as a stable pattern. It will build into numerous probable realities, any number of which can be activated at any time, providing the contingencies for the individual's death. In effect, breaking the spell necessitates a countervailing hex to neutralize the alien thought form from becoming fully activated as a stable organizing state. Significantly, Lee Gandee mentions that "anyone with enough faith to break a spell is not subject to a spell in the first place."

While often enormous energy is used to harm someone, the same kind of process can be used to shore up another individual's health, provide encouragement with positive thoughts, and delicate guidance when it appears that someone's thought field is becoming overpowered. In addition, there are numerous love hexes, charms against demons, spells against disease, and even hymns for virility to be found in all cultures. In this respect, *each human interaction can be viewed in part as a hexing process.*

129

While the broadcasting of good or bad feelings may not be normally generated in the same way as a concentrated hex, human interchange nonetheless potentially provides each individual with one information-processing dilemma—or opportunity—after another.

Many individuals are considered exceptionally "sensitive." This may mean that an individual with a greater awareness of another's probable realities becomes more alert to that individual's needs and desires. The well-focused information processor may almost totally lack compassion. I am suggesting there is no such thing as telepathic communication apart from our everyday life. We are part of and contributors to an ongoing, ever-changing matrix of *behavior*. Each person contributes uniquely to it, and continuously activates certain thoughts over others and stabilizes them as constructs of physical reality. Breaking a habitual focus of consciousness, thus impairing stabilized thought, brings us in tune with other thought patterns which exist in different degrees of vitality. Telepathic reception, in effect, means opening ourselves up to probable realities as they are generated by others, as well as to the concentrated thoughts of others which remain accessible to us, depending on how flexible our individual information processing becomes.

Harold Sherman is famous for participating in one of the most dramatic telepathy experiments, in which he communicated with Arctic explorer Sir Hubert Wilkins at a distance of 3,400 miles, Sherman has a number of practical instructions to improve telepathic reception and transmission, believing that relaxation is necessary to the point that we become almost totally unaware of the existence of the physical body. This can be done by allowing the conscious mind to travel from toe to head, almost dissolving each part of our existence as it travels upward. Sherman's technique involves visualizing a blank motion-picture screen and attempting to transmit our thoughts to it. Reception of telepathic images involves keeping this screen blank and waiting for strong indications of images as well as feelings.

Andrija Puharich believes that the word "sender" is really a misnomer. Puharich claims that the sender *draws* the receiver, creating a kind of mental vacuum to which the receiver's mind is tuned. The sender, according to Puharich, is generally in a high state of excitement. The sympathetic nervous system becomes dominant and acts antagonistically towards the parasympathetic system. Heartbeat accelerates and the body is prepared for considerable exertion. When the sympathetic system is activated by adrenalin and related adrenalin type compounds, this state is called *adrenergia*. The receiver, on the other hand, is generally in a state of *cholinergia*. What Sherman and Puharich are describing is a type of information exchange which I believe, like hexing, is a continuous process involving everyone, everywhere.

VI. POSSESSION AND POLTERGEISTS

I believe that something similar occurs with what is generally known as possession. The probable realities that have been created by an individual may be so strong that they form energy gestalts which become increasingly ready to invade the individual's information field and challenge the dominant focus of consciousness.

In a sense, the individual himself becomes the so-called "possessing form" in that more routinized behavior is now occupying a different level of reality in that individual's multidimensional organizing state. In *The Devils of Loudun,* detailing one of the most famous cases of demonic possession involving nuns of a small convent in the seventeenth-century French town, Aldous Huxley presented a similar view. He believed that possession was a form of self-transcendance. People sought to escape from being themselves and a devil or spirit was a vehicle

131

for such an escape. More recently, in an introduction to his anthology on exorcism, Martin Ebon had this to say:

> *Self-dramatization, serious emotional imbalance, a psychological "opening up" and outside influences—sometime through drugs or psycho-physiological exercises—can be factors leading to symptoms of possession. We know too little about psychosomatic factors, even in such illnesses as headaches, stomach pains or skin rashes, to speak with any sort of certainty about possession cases. But there exists a strong element of cultural expectation; of that we can be sure. And I do not doubt that the right kind of exorcism, performed within the appropriate setting, can indeed "drive out" an emotional and psycho-physiological illness that may dramatize itself in a personalized manner.*

The process of exorcism, therefore, can be seen primarily as a means of reestablishing and regrouping the thought patterns that constitute the previously dominant everyday range of consciousness of the "possessed" individual.

This "psychiatric" enforcement, however, can be dangerous. According to John Pearce-Higgins, clergy called in to exorcise can do considerable damage, since the Church represents moral authority. He believes that many of the cases signify a strong challenge and protest against authority, and any solemn rites performed may only serve to augment the nature of the possession. The Roman ritual issued in 1619, for example, involves twenty-three pages of solemn exorcist rites involving the use of prayers and psalm readings, as well as passages from the Gospel. Historically, it has been acknowledged that an act of exorcism involved a considerable risk to the exorcist, for he might become possessed himself. In some of the more classical cases of possession where sexuality appeared to be the dominant theme, it was believed that the priest himself could be seduced by a demon using the body of a woman.

Recently possession has been linked to poltergeist phenomena. A quite literal translation of poltergeist, a German word, is "noisy ghost." William G. Roll has recently attributed poltergeist phenomena to individuals· who have great difficulty at verbal expression. Often the poltergeist phenomena is very antisocial, and this may be a vehicle enabling the poltergeist agent to unleash his fury at another level of his organizing state.

One poltergeist manifestation which has been extensively investigated is the poltergeist fire. Often a piece of clothing catches on fire, a curtain, a piece of paper; it is believed that this phenomenon is set off by a powerful act of mind. One story reported by Vincent H. Gaddis, in *Mysterious Fires and Lights* gives us a good idea of its nature:

> *Early one morning late in February 1959 Mr. and Mrs. George Byrnes were awakened in their Miami, Florida, home by the screams of their daughter, 14-year-old Evelyn. The girl had been sleeping in the living room, and her bedclothing was on fire. She helped her parents drag the smoldering bedding into the front yard. On returning to the house the Byrnes discovered that the living room curtains, about eight feet from the bed, were aflame, so were the curtains in the adjoining dining room and kitchen. After these blazes had been extinguished, the family found that the curtains were burning in an enclosed patio, separated from the rest of the house by a closed door. Some of these kinds of blazes destroy or damage buildings, but most of them seem concentrated on small objects. Curtains and drapes appear to be primary targets.*

According to George Owen, a veteran poltergeist investigator, these fires may be a result of a strong release of vital energy that speeds up molecular agitation in a target object. Owen has written: "If we admit that forces exist which vibrate solids so that they produce sounds,

133

then it is hard to see any limitations." This release of energy, I suggest, is activated through a pattern of information processing which suddenly focuses almost completely on unanswered drives of an increasingly charged aspect of "self."

Chapter Nine

Psychics and Psychic Phenomena: Some Closing Critical Remarks

During the last two years I have often found myself confronting people who announce that they have psychic abilities and who proceed to demonstrate their talent to make predictions, very often without being asked. On one occasion, I had been doing research at the Parapsychology Foundation Library in New York when I was approached by a man of about twenty-five, bearded, shabbily dressed, with an air of arrogance characterizing his overall disposition. He stared at me for at least a minute and then announced that I wasn't "clear enough yet," that I was holding back my psychic ability and that if I unleashed it, I could be "a good medium."

From past experience, I immediately suspected that he was about to plug a treatment or learning program where I could get "clear" and become an overnight psychic success story. But his intentions were even more oppressive. He introduced himself as a well-known psychic from California, who often did psychic healing. Without my

135

request, he decided to give me a medical analysis which seemed terribly confused, rambling, and uncertain. Not only was he inarticulate, but he continued this assault even after I had asked him to stop.

At a time when more people are beginning to believe that there are methods of tapping more information, this kind of information assault is unfortunately becoming more common. The need to impress often overrides any carefully-thought-out way to present others with subtle glimpses of information which may affect them in some way. My friend Matt, for example, is slowly learning to "read" people, but in no way does he attempt to impose his information processing on anyone. He will offer his impressions if he is asked, but even then, if he receives some strong impressions about his subject, he will never scream "fire." Very subtly and indirectly Matt will turn the subject's attention to the relevant issues. This often enables the subject to make a *self*-discovery, so to speak, and therefore has a much more sound a base from which to alter behavior which may be potentially dangerous. A couple of times Matt has processed death imagery about someone and was less subtle and more direct in his guidance. At other times he might sound out his subject about how willing he might be to discuss a particular issue. If he gets an impression about a financial crisis, for example, he may at some point in the conversation provide a personal story of how he dealt with a personal financial fiasco. Matt has used this approach with me regarding a number of his impressions about my life and has slipped a few hints from time to time. Once he made me do a double take because I couldn't figure out why he suddenly changed a topic. But at least in this particular case, it was still a much more sensitive way of telling me something than generating unnecessary excitement and fear.

From the standpoint of information processing, I speculated earlier that a correct prediction essentially involves a person's stop-action view of an individual's dominant self, or a much wider organizing state such as a dominant societal state. A person also may detect other aspects of his subject's evolving "self" and be capable of projecting what may occur if this "aspect" emerges and radically restructures the individual's dominant organizing state. On the other hand, when impressions are received by someone like Matt, it is entirely possible that he may be picking out probable realities which may have little chance of becoming manifest at the physical level, particularly if the individual becomes more aware of these states and makes a strong effort to behave differently. Unfortunately, the tendency to believe in the inevitability of certain predictions can often be a very haunting and fearful experience for an individual. In fact, the acceptance of a prediction may operate very much like a hex, fixating the individual at that level of reality. The fact that some predictions may be very accurate due to an individual's laserlike quality of mind in certain circumstances, however, should not be discounted. The problem is that there is simply no way of deciphering what level of the matrix the impressions are from. But even if this were known, there would still be no guarantee that the evolution of the matrix and the individual's information processing could be accurately charted. When we are dealing with the continuity of mental states on a mass level and the synergistic information exchange involved along each person's multidimensional energy continuum, a completely accurate prediction at any given point is not necessarily a guide to what may be in the process of happening but just as likely an indication of what might happen if certain matrix configurations persist or recur. While I believe that certain approximations may be deducted, I'm suggesting that the entire state of matrix evolution can never be accurately described all at once.

While the universal information matrix is seen as evolving in accordance with laws of order which themselves are evolving, there is no standard, no static conception, no rules, guidelines which are anything more

137

than information being processed, and activated on the material and more subtle planes or dimensions of the self and of the society at any given time. While human behavior may appear routinized and hence predictable, this is completely illusory, and a function of how we differentially activate this behavior. Our morals, laws, customs, institutions, political structures are all therefore dynamically organizing, never static, and processed at different states of reality.

A scientific attempt to make sense of human behavior is itself an organizing system of making what the late Alan Watts once described as "fixity out of flux." Even though a number of parapsychologists have recently been advocating that scientific work be conducted from the actual experience of numerous "altered states of consciousness," in terms of information processing, this is at best only a method of becoming more personally aware of other aspects of one's self, and should not be confused with the more traditional belief that an "out-there" reality can be "objectively" codified or explained. In this context the scientist becomes a human being again, removes himself from a lofty tower of "objective" observation apart from his own information processing and a world that everybody contributes to and shares at one level or another.

I want to make it very clear at this point that I do not wish to discourage scientific activity. Rather, I would like to see more humility become prevalent in this enterprise and a greater appreciation of what appears to be involved in any kind of codification. In addition, a less culture-bound awareness of the diversity of human activity in a universal context would, I feel, be more sobering for people who desire to collect information and use it, in turn, to instruct others.

However, I am not naïve enough to pretend that this is the trend in modern parapsychology. If anything, the tendency is to reify procedure rather than extend experience, and to create a new intellectual monopoly dictating

138

what conceptual parameters constitute a "correct" way of exploring human potential. To those who would insist that the only way that greater numbers of people will accept parapsychological research will be through a tightening of scientific method and a saturation campaign of testing anyone who appears gifted, I can only respond that they have relied much too heavily on *one* system of experiencing the world. And in their persistence to validate "psychic occurrences" have paradoxically contributed to a mass audience's preoccupation with sensationalistic tales of the impossible.

The Road Back to Danville

Almost two years after visiting the dowsers at Danville to watch them find deep and shallow wells, lost coins, and exhibit the very latest of dowsing equipment, I am ready to return—only this time, for very different reasons. Danville, in a very personal way, has become a symbol of the contrasting realities, the subtle but important differences in a culture in which uniformity is rampant and regions of the mind wait in abeyance to be explored.

In the last two years, there has been a noticeable change in public attitude toward attempts to examine what these mysteries may hold for our collective future on this planet and what extensions of "self" can be practically applied in our everyday lives. There is good reason to be enthusiastic about this new mood, but there is an equally good reason to attempt to understand all that is happening in the widest context possible, lest we merely re-create old antagonisms toward even more novel exploration. And without a doubt, there are dangers. Human history seems to carry an archetypal self-destruct mechanism which lies at the periphery of all progress.

Places like Danville offer moments to scan this periphery because they are not only peaceful retreats from the fast-paced madness, but are *states of mind* where new adventures begin . . . and so the odyssey continues.

141

Bibliography

The Academy of Parapsychology and Medicine, *The Dimensions of Healing*. Los Altos, California: Transcript of a symposium at Stanford University, September 30-October 3, 1972 and at the University of California at Los Angeles, October 5-8, 1972.

————, *The Varieties of Healing Experience: Exploring Psychic Phenomena in Healing*. Los Altos, California: Transcript of the Interdisciplinary Symposium of October 30, 1971.

ADAMENKO, V.G., *"Electrodynamics of Living Systems,"* Journal of Paraphysics, 4: 1970.

ADAMSKI, GEORGE, *Inside the Flying Saucers*. New York: Warner Paperback Library. 1967.

ALDER, VERA STANLEY, *The Fifth Dimension*, rev. ed. London: Rider & Co., 1970.

ALFVÉN, HANNES, "Antimatter and Cosmology," *Scientific American*, 216:4, 1967.

————, *Worlds-Antiworlds: Antimatter in Cosmology*. San Francisco: W.H. Freeman & Co., 1966.

ALTSCHULER, RICHARD, and NICHOLAS M. REGUSH, *Open Reality*. New York: G.P. Putnam's Sons, 1974.

ANDERSON, N., *The Electromagnetic Field*. New York: Plenum Press, 1968.

ANDERSON, PAUL, *Is There Life on Other Worlds?* New York: Collier Books, 1968.

ARKLE, WILLIAM, *A Geography of Consciousness*. London: Neville Spearman, 1974.

ARROW, JAY, "Radioastronomy Today," *Vertex* 1:4, 1973.

ASIMOV, ISAAC, "I Can't Believe I Saw the Whole Thing!" *Saturday Review of Science*, September 2, 1972.

BACKSTER, C., "Evidence of a Primary Perception in Plant Life," *International Journal of Parapsychology*, 10:4, 1968.

BAGNALL, OSCAR, *The Origin and Properties of the Human Aura.* New York: University Books, 1970.

BAKER, DOUGLAS M., *The Techniques of Astral Projection.* London: Regency Press, n.d.

BARBER, T.X., "Death by Suggestion: A Critical Note," *Psychosomatic Medicine, 23:* 1961.

BARCLAY, GLEN, *Mind Over Matter.* New York: Bobbs-Merrill, 1973.

BARNETT, LINCOLN, *The Universe and Dr. Einstein.* New York: Bantam Books, 1968.

BARNOTHY, MADELEINE F. ed., *Biological Effects of Magnetic Fields.* New York: Plenum Press, 1964.

BARRETT, WILLIAM, and THEODORE BESTERMAN, *The Divining Rod: An Experimental and Psychological Investigation.* New York: University Books, 1968.

BEAL, JAMES B., "Paraphysics and Parapsychology," *Analog,* April 1973.

BEANE, MARY, "Super Oxygen—The Promises and Plain Truth," *Prevention,* July 1973.

BEAU, GEORGES, *Chinese Medicine.* New York: Avon Books, 1972.

BECKER, ROBERT, "Relationship of a Geo-Magnetic Environment to Human Biology," *New York State Journal of Medicine,* 63:15, 1963.

BELL, A.H., *Practical Dowsing—A Symposium.* London: G. Bell & Sons, 1965.

BERGSON, HENRI, *Duration and Simultaneity.* New York: Bobbs-Merrill, 1965.

————, *Matter and Memory.* London: Allen and Unwin, 1950.

————, *Mind-Energy.* New York: Henry Holt & Co., 1920.

BERLITZ, CHARLES, *Mysteries from Forgotten Worlds.* New York: Dell, 1973.

144

BERNSTEIN, MOREY, *The Search for Bridey Murphy.* New York: Lancer Books, n.d.

BESANT, ANNIE, and C.W. LEADBEATER, *Thought-Forms.* Wheaton, Illinois: The Theosophical Publishing House, 1969.

Bioenergetic Questions. Material of the Scientific Methodological Seminar in Alma-Ata, 1969. Southern California Society for Psychical Research.

BIRD, CHRISTOPHER, "Dowsing in the U.S.A.: History, Achievement and Current Research," *The American Dowser,* August 1973.

————, "Dowsing in the U.S.S.R.," *The American Dowser,* August 1972.

BLAIR, RICHARD, "Firewalkers of Mt. Takao," *Probe—The Unknown,* August 1973.

BLAVATSKY, H.P., *The Secret Doctrine: The Synthesis of Science, Religion and Philosophy,* Vols. I and II. Pasadena, California: Theosophical University Press, 1970.

BLEIBTRAU, JOHN N., *The Parable of the Beast.* New York: Collier Books, 1971.

BLEICH, ALAN RALPH, *The Story of X rays: From Röntgen to Isotopes.* New York: Dover Publications, n.d.

BLUM, RALPH and JUDY BLUM, *Beyond Earth: Man's Contact With UFOs.* New York: Bantam Books, 1974.

BLUMRICH, JOSEF F., *The Space Ships of Ezekiel.* New York: Bantam Books, 1974.

BOADELLA, DAVID, *Wilhelm Reich: The Evolution of His Work.* Chicago: Henry Regnery, 1974.

BOEHME, JACOB, *Six Theosophic Points.* Ann Arbor, Michigan: University of Michigan Press, 1958.

BOHM, DAVID, *Causality and Chance in Modern Physics.* New York: Van Nostrand, 1957.

————, "Quantum Theory as an Indication of a New Legal Order in Physics, Part A," *Foundations of Physics,* 1:4, 1971.

BOLEN, JAMES GRAYSON, "Interview: Shafica Karagulla, M.D.," *Psychic*, July-August 1973.

————, "Interview: Harold Sherman," *Psychic*, January-February 1974.

BOLEN, JEAN S., "Meditation and Psychotherapy in the Treatment of Cancer," *Psychic*, July-August 1973.

BRAGDON, CLAUDE, *A Primer of Higher Space: The Fourth Dimension.* Tucson, Arizona: Owen Press, 1972.

BRAMWELL, JAMES, *Lost Atlantis.* New York: Freeway Press, 1973.

BRENA, STEPHEN F., *Yoga and Medicine.* Baltimore: Pelican, 1973.

BRENNAN, J.H., *The Occult Reich.* New York: New American Library, 1974.

BRO, HARMON H., *Edgar Cayce on Dreams.* New York: Paperback Library, 1968.

BROMAGE, BERNARD, *The Occult Arts of Ancient Egypt.* New York: Samuel Weiser, n.d.

BROWN, FRANK A., *Biological Clocks.* Boston: American Institute of Biological Sciences, 1962.

————, "How Animals Respond to Magnetism," *Discovery*, November, 1963.

————, "Persistent Activity Rhythms in the Oyster," *American Journal of Physiology*, 178:510, 1954.

————, "Response to Pervasive Geophysical Factors and the Biological Clock Problem," Cold Spring Harbor Symposia in *Quantitative Biology*, 25: 1960.

BROWN, G. SPENCER, *Laws of Form.* New York: Julian Press, 1973.

BROWN, ROSEMARY, *Unfinished Symphonies: The Amazing Story of a World-Famous Medium.* London: Pan Books, 1973.

BROWN, SLATER, *The Heyday of Spiritualism.* New York: Pocket Books, 1972.

BROWNING, NORMA LEE, *The Psychic World of Peter Hurkos*. New York: New American Library, 1971.

BRUNER, JEROME, *On Knowing: Essay for the Left Hand*. Cambridge, Mass.: Harvard University Press, 1962.

_____, "On Perceptual Readiness," *Psychological Review*, 64: 1957.

_____, and Leo Postman, "On the Perception of Incongruity: A Paradigm," *Journal of Personality*, 18: 1949.

BRUNTON, PAUL, *The Hidden Teaching Beyond Yoga*. London: Rider & Co., 1969.

_____, *A Search in Secret Egypt*. London: Rider & Co., 1969.

_____, *A Search in Secret India*. London: Rider & Co., 1970.

_____, *The Wisdom of the Overself*. New York: Samuel Weiser, 1972.

BUCKE, RICHARD MORRIS, *Cosmic Consciousness, a Study in the Evolution of the Human Mind*. New York: E.P. Dutton & Co., 1948.

BUDGE, E. A. WALLIS *The Egyptian Book of the Dead*. New York: Dover Publications, 1967.

BURCKHARDT, TITUS, *Alchemy: Science of the Cosmos, Science of the Soul*. Baltimore: Penguin, 1971.

BURKS, ARTHUR J., *The Aura*. Lakemont, Georgia: CSA Printers and Publishers, 1962.

BURR, H.S., "Biological Organization and the Cancer Problem," *Yale Journal of Biology and Medicine*, 12:281, 1940.

_____, *Blueprint for Immortality: The Electric Patterns of Life*. London: Neville Spearman, 1972.

_____, "Effect of Severe Storms on Electrical Properties of a Tree and the Earth," *Science*, 124:1204, 1956.

_____, "Field Properties of the Developing Frog's Egg," *Proceedings of the National Academy of Science*, 27:276. 1941.

_____, and F.S.C. Northrup, "The Electrodynamic Theory of Life," *Quarterly Review of Biology*, 10:322, 1935.

————, and L. Langman, "Electrometric Timing of Human Ovulation," *American Journal of Obstetrics and Gynaecology,* 44:223, 1942.

CAMERON, VERNE L., *Aquavideo: Locating Underground Water,* Bill Cox, ed. Elsinore, California: El Cariso Publications, 1970.

————, *Map Dowsing,* Bill Cox and Georgiana Teeple, eds. Elsinore, California: El Cariso Publications, 1971.

————, *Oil Locating,* Bill Cox and Georgiana Teeple, eds., Elsinore, California: El Cariso Publications, 1971.

CAMP, JOHN, *Magic, Myth and Medicine.* New York: Taplinger, 1973.

CAMPBELL, JOHN, "Unprovable Speculation," *Astounding Science Fiction,* February 1957.

CANNON, W.B., "Voodoo Death," *American Anthropologist,* 44: 1942.

CARREL, ALEXIS, *Man the Unknown.* New York: Harper & Brothers, 1939.

CARRINGTON, HEREWARD, *The Psychic World.* New York: G.P. Putnam's Sons, 1937.

CARTER, MARY ELLEN, and WILLIAM A. McGAREY, *Edgar Cayce on Healing.* New York: Paperback Library, 1972.

————, *Edgar Cayce on Prophecy.* New York: Paperback Library, 1968.

CASTANEDA, CARLOS, *The Teachings of Don Juan.* Berkeley: University of California Press, 1968.

CAVENDER, KENNETH, "Voyage of the Psychenauts," *Harper's,* January 1974.

CAVENDISH, RICHARD, *The Black Arts.* New York: Capricorn Books, 1968.

————, *Encyclopedia of the Unexplained: Magic, Occultism and Parapsychology.* London: Routledge and Kegan Paul, 1974.

CAYCE, EDGAR, *Auras.* Virginia Beach: ARE Press, 1945.

CAYCE, EDGAR EVANS, *Edgar Cayce on Atlantis.* New York: Paperback Library, 1968.

_____, and Hugh Lynn Cayce, *The Outer Limits of Edgar Cayce's Power.* New York: Harper & Row, 1973.

CAYCE, HUGH LYNN, *Venture Inward.* New York: Paperback Library, 1966.

CERMINARA, GINA, *Insights for the Age of Aquarius: A Scientific Analysis of the Problems of Religion.* Englewood Cliffs, New Jersey: Prentice-Hall, 1973.

_____, *Many Mansions.* New York: New American Library, 1967.

CHARROUX, ROBERT, *The Mysterious Unknown.* London: Neville Spearman, 1972.

CHELTHAM, ERIKA, *The Prophecies of Nostradamus.* New York: G.P. Putnam's Sons, 1974.

CLEMENT, MARK, *The Waves that Heal: The New Science of Radio Biology.* Rustington, Sussex, England: Health Science Press, 1965.

COLLIN, RODNEY, *The Theory of Celestial Influence.* New York: Samuel Weiser, 1973.

CONE, C.D. and M. TONGIER, Jr., "Control of Somatic Cell Mitosis by Simulated Changes in the Transmembrane Potential Level," *Oncology*, 25: 1971.

COX, WILLIAM E., "Parapsychology and Magicians," *Parapsychology Review*, 5:3, 1974.

CRENSHAW, JAMES, "Uri Geller: Space Age 'Magician,' " *Fate*, January 1974.

CRILE, GEORGE WASHINGTON, *The Bipolar Theory of Living Processes.* New York: Macmillan, 1926.

CROOKALL, ROBERT, *The Mechanisms of Astral Projection: Denouement After Seventy Years.* Moradabad, India: Darshana International, 1969.

149

_____, *Study and Practice of Astral Projection.* New York: University Books, 1966.

CUMONT, FRANZ, *Astrology and Religion Among The Greeks and Romans.* New York: Dover Publications, 1960.

DAKIN, H.S., High-Voltage Photography, 3456 Jackson Street, San Francisco, 94118, 1974.

DARWIN, CHARLES, *The Origin of Species.* New York: Collier Books, 1962.

DAUVEN, JEAN, *The Powers of Hypnosis.* New York: Stein & Day, 1971.

DAVIS, ALBERT ROY, and A.K. BHATTACHARYA, *Magnet and Magnetic Fields, or Healing by Magnets.* Calcutta: Firma K.L. Mukhopadhyay, 1970.

DAY, G.W. LANGSTON, and GEORGE DE LA WARR, *Matter in the Making.* London: Stuart, 1966.

_____, *New Worlds Beyond the Atom.* London: Stuart, 1956.

DEAN, E. DOUGLAS, "The Plethysmograph as an Indicator of ESP," *Journal of the Society for Psychical Research,* 41: 1962.

DeBONO, EDWARD, *The Use of Lateral Thinking.* Harmondsworth, Middlesex, England: Pelican, 1971.

DeCAMP, L. SPRAGUE, *The Ancient Engineers.* New York: Ballantine, 1974.

DeROPP, ROBERT S., *Drugs and the Mind.* New York: Grove Press, 1957.

_____, *The Master Game.* New York: Delta, 1968.

_____, *The New Prometheans.* New York: Delta, 1973.

DONNELLY, IGNATIUS, *Atlantis: The Antediluvian World.* Blauvelt, New York: Rudolf Steiner Publications, 1971.

_____, *The Destruction of Atlantis: Ragnarök: The Age of Fire and Gravel,* Blauvelt, New York: Rudolf Steiner Publications, 1971.

DOOLEY, ANNE, *Every Wall a Door: Exploring Psychic Surgery and Healing.* London: Abelard-Schuman, 1973.

DUCASSE, C.J., *Paranormal Phenomena, Science and Life After Death.* New York: Parapsychology Foundation, Monograph No. 8, 1969.

DUNNE, J.W., *An Experiment With Time.* London: A. and C. Black, 1929.

EBON, MARTIN, ed., *Exorcism: Fact Not Fiction.* New York: New American Library, 1974.

————, *Prophecy in Our Time.* North Hollywood, California: Wilshire Book Co., 1971.

————, ed., *Psychic Discoveries by the Russians.* New York: New American Library, 1971.

————, *They Knew the Unknown.* New York: World Publishing Co., 1971.

EDDINGTON, A.S., *The Nature of the Physical World.* New York: The Macmillan Co., 1929.

EDEN, JEROME, trans., *Maxims on Animal Magnetism by F.A. Mesmer.* Mount Vernon, New York: The Eden Press, 1958.

————, *Orgone Energy.* New York: Vantage Press, 1972.

EDSON, LEE, "A Secret Weapon Called Immunology," *The New York Times Magazine,* February 17, 1974.

EDWARDS, HARRY, *The Healing Intelligence.* New York: Hawthorn, n.d.

EHRENWALD, J., "Telepathy and the Child-Parent Relationship," *Journal of the American Society for Psychical Research,* 48: 1954.

————, *Telepathy and Medical Psychology.* New York: Norton, 1948.

EISENBUD, JULE, *PSI and Psychoanalysis.* New York: Grune & Stratton, 1970.

————, *The World of Ted Serios.* New York: William Morrow, 1967.

ELIADE, MIRCEA, *The Forge and the Crucible: The Origins and Structures of Alchemy.* New York: Harper & Row, 1971.

151

————, *Rites and Symbols of Initiation*. New York: Harper & Row, 1965.

ELLIS, DAVID, "Tape Recordings from the Dead?" *Psychic,* January-February, 1974.

EMMONS, VIVA, *The Roots of Peace.* Wheaton, Illinois: The Theosophical Publishing House, 1969.

FAGAN, CYRIL, Astrological Origins. St. Paul, Minnesota: Llewellyn Publications, 1973.

FEINBERG, LEONARD, "Fire Walking in Ceylon," *The Atlantic Monthly,* 203: 1959.

FERGUSON, MARILYN, *The Brain Revolution.* New York: Taplinger, 1973.

FODOR, NANDOR, *The Haunted Mind.* New York: Signet Books, 1968.

FORT, CHARLES, *The Book of the Damned.* New York: Ace Books, n.d.

————, *Lo!* New York: Ace Books, n.d.

————, *New Lands.* New York: Ace Books, n.d.

FORWARD, HAAKON, *Mind, Matter and Gravitation.* New York: Parapsychology Foundation, Monograph No. 11, 1969.

FOUCAULT, MICHEL, *Madness and Civilization: A History of Insanity in the Age of Reason.* New York: Vintage Books, 1973.

FOX, OLIVER, *Astral Projection.* New York: University Books, 1962.

FRASER, J.T., ed., *The Voices of Time.* New York: George Braziller, 1966.

FREEDLAND, NAT., *The Occult Explosion.* New York: Berkley Publishing Corp., 1972.

FREEMAN, JAMES M., "Trial by Fire," *Natural History,* January 1974.

FREUD, SIGMUND, "Dreams and Telepathy" in *Collected Papers,* Vol. IV. New York: Basic Books, 1959.

152

————, *The Interpretation of Dreams.* London: Allen & Unwin, 1954.

FULLER, JOHN G., *Arigo: Surgeon of the Rusty Knife.* New York: Thomas Y. Crowell, 1974.

————, *The Great Soul Trial.* New York: Macmillan, 1969.

————, *Incident at Exeter: Unidentified Flying Objects Over America Now.* New York: Berkley Publishing Corp., 1967.

————, *The Interrupted Journey.* New York: Berkley Publishing Corp., 1974.

FULLER, R. BUCKMINSTER, *Intuition.* New York: Doubleday, 1972.

FURST, JEFFREY, *Edgar Cayce's Story of Attitudes and Emotions.* New York: Coward, McCann & Geoghegan, 1972.

GADDIS, VINCENT H., *Mysterious Fires and Lights.* New York: David Mackay & Co., 1967.

GALE, RICHARD M., ed., *The Philosophy of Time: A Collection of Essays.* New York: Doubleday-Anchor, 1967.

GALLERT, MARK L., *New Light on Therapeutic Energies.* London: James Clarke & Co., 1966.

GANDEE, LEE R., *Strange Experience: An Autobiography of a Hexenmeister—Personal Encounters with Hauntings, Magic and Mysticism.* Englewood Cliffs, New Jersey: Prentice-Hall, 1973.

GARDNER, MARTIN, *Fads and Fallacies in the Name of Science.* New York: Dover Publications, 1957.

————, "What Hath Hoova Wrought?" *The New York Review,* May 16, 1974.

GARRETT, EILEEN J., *Awareness.* New York: Berkley Publishing Corp., 1968.

————, *The Sense and Nonsense of Prophecy.* New York: Berkley Publishing Corp., 1968.

————, *Telepathy.* New York: Creative Age Press, 1945.

GARVIN, RICHARD, *The Crystal Skull.* New York: Pocket Books, 1974.

GASTER, THEODOR H., ed., *The New Golden Bough* (abridged from the classic work by Sir James Frazer). New York: The New American Library, 1964.

GAULD, ALAN, *The Founders of Psychical Research*. New York: Schocken, 1968.

GAUQUELIN, MICHEL, *The Cosmic Clocks*. London: Peter Owen, 1969.

————, *The Scientific Basis of Astrology*. New York: Stein & Day, 1969.

GILLIE, OLIVER, *The Living Cell*. London: Thames & Hudson, 1971.

GOODAVAGE, JOSEPH F., *Astrology, the Space-Age Science*. West Nyack, New York: Parker Publishing Co., 1966.

————, "Contact With Extraterrestrial Life." *Saga*, January 1973.

GOVINDA, LAMA ANGARIKA, *The Way of the White Clouds: The Buddhist Pilgrim in Tibet*. Berkeley, California: Shambala Publications, 1970.

GRAD, BERNARD, R.J. CADORET, and G.I. PAUL, "The Influence of an Unorthodox Method Treatment on Wound Healing of Mice," *International Journal of Parapsychology*, 3:5, 1961.

————, "The Laying-on-of-Hands: Implications for Psychotherapy, Gentling and the Placebo Effect," *Journal of the American Society for Psychical Research*, 61:286, 1967.

————, "Some Biological Effects of the Laying-on-of-Hands," *Journal of the American Society for Psychical Research*, 59:2, 1965.

————, "A Telekinetic Effect on Plant Growth," *International Journal of Parapsychology*, 6:473, 1964.

GREGORY, R.L., *The Intelligent Eye*. London: Weidenfeld & Nicolson, 1971.

GREEN, ELMER, ALICE GREEN and E. WALTERS, "Voluntary Control of Internal States: Psychological and Physiological," *Journal of Transpersonal Psychology*, 1: 1970.

154

GREENBERG, DANIEL S.,"The French Concoction," *Saturday Review of Science*, n.d.

GUÉNON, RENÉ, *The Reign of Quantity and the Signs of the Times*. Baltimore: Penguin, 1972.

GURVICH, ALEKSANDR G., *Mitogenetic Radiation: Physicochemical Bases and Applications in Biology and Medicine* (in Russian). Moscow: Medgiz, 1945.

HALACY, DANIEL S., JR., *Radiation, Magnetism and Living Things*. New York: Holiday House, 1966.

HALL, CALVIN, *The Meaning of Dreams*. New York: Dell, 1959.

HANSEL, C.E.M., *ESP: A Scientific Evaluation*. New York: Charles Scribner's Sons, 1966.

HARDY, ALISTER, ROBERT HARVIE, AND ARTHUR KOESTLER, *The Challenge of Chance: A Mass Experiment in Telepathy and Its Unexpected Outcome*. New York: Random House, 1974.

HARKER, J.E., "Diurnal Rhythms in Periplaneta Americana L.," *Nature*, *173:689*, 1954.

————, *The Physiology of Diurnal Rhythms*. London: Cambridge University Press, 1964.

HARNER, MICHAEL J., ed., *Hallucinogen and Shamanism*. New York: Oxford University Press, 1973.

HARVALIK, Z.V., "The Biophysical Magnetometer-Gradiometer," *The Virginia Journal of Science*, 21: 1970.

HAWKING, S.W., AND G.F.R. ELLIS, *The Large-Scale Structure of Space-Time*. New York: Cambridge University Press, 1973.

HAWKINS, GERALD S., AND JOHN B. WHITE, *Stonehenge Decoded*. New York: Delta, n.d.

HAYNES, MARGUERITE, *The Magic and Power of Symbols*. New York: Award Books, 1970.

HAYNES, RENÉE, *The Hidden Springs: An Enquiry into Extrasensory Perception*. rev. ed. New York: Little-Brown, 1973.

HEAD, JOSEPH, AND S.L. CRANSTON, *Reincarnation: An East-West Anthology.* Wheaton, Illinois: The Theosophical Publishing House, 1968.

Health Research, *The Aura and What It Means to You: A Compilation from Many Authorities.* Mokelumne Hill, California: Health Research, 1955.

Hearings Before the Committee on Science and Astronautics, U.S. House of Representatives, 90th Congress, second session, July 29, 1968. *Symposium on Unidentified Flying Objects.*

HENDRIX, CHARLES E., "Possible Effects of External Electric and Magnetic Shields on the Human Nervous System," prepared for: U.S. Army Advanced Material Concepts Agency, Washington, D.C.

HERBERT, B., "Report on Nina Kulagina," *Parapsychology Review,* 3:6, 1972.

HERBERT, FRANK, "Listening to the Left Hand: The Dangerous Business of Wishing for Absolutes in a Relativistic Universe," *Harper's,* December 1973.

HEYWOOD, ROSALIND, *The Sixth Sense.* rev. ed. London: Pan Books, 1971.

HIERONYMOUS, LOUISE AND GALEN, "Tracking the Astronauts in Apollo XI with Data from Apollo VIII Included. A Quantitative Evaluation of the Well-Being of the Three Men through the Period from Two Days Before Lift-Off Until the Quarantine Ended—A Consolidated Report." Privately published, September 4, 1969.

HILLMAN, W.S., "Injury of Tomato Plants by Continuous Light and Unfavorable Photoperiodic Cycles." *American Journal of Botany,* 43: 89, 1956.

HOLZER, HANS, *Psychic Photography: Threshold of a New Science?* New York: McGraw-Hill, 1969.

HORN, PATRICIA, and the editors of *Behavior Today,* "A Case Study: Hex Death in Baltimore," *Psychology Today,* March 1973.

HUGHES, PENNETHORNE, *Witchcraft.* London: Pelican Books, 1967.

156

HUXLEY, ALDOUS, *The Devils of Loudun.* London: Penguin Books, 1971.

_____ , *The Doors of Perception and Heaven and Hell.* New York: Harper & Row, 1954.

HYNEK, J. ALLEN, *The UFO Experience: A Scientific Inquiry.* New York: Ballantine, 1974.

IDLER, RUSS, "Planets Give us a Charge!" *Probe—The Unknown,* June 1973.

INGLIS, BRIAN, *Fringe Medicine.* London: Faber and Faber, 1964.

INGRAHAM, B.V., *Meditation in the Silence.* Lee's Summit, Missouri: Unity School of Christianity, 1969.

INYUSHIN, V.M., "Biological Plasma of Human Organism with Animals," *Telepathy, Telegnosis, Dowsing, Psychokinesis,* Prague: Svoboda, 1970.

JACO, E. GARTLEY, *Patients, Physicians and Illness: Behavioral Science and Medicine.* Glencoe, Illinois: The Free Press, 1963.

JACOBSON, NILS O., *Life Without Death? On Parapsychology, Mysticism and the Question of Survival.* New York: Delacorte/Seymour Lawrence, 1974.

JAMES, TREVOR, *They Live in the Sky!* Los Angeles, California: New Age Publishing Co., 1958.

JAMES, WILLIAM, *The Varieties of Religious Experience.* New York: New American Library, 1958.

JEANS, J., *The Mysterious Universe.* New York: Dover Publications, 1968.

JENNINGS, JOAN, "Health Requires Natural Light," *Prevention,* September 1973.

JOHNSON, RAYNOR C., *The Imprisoned Splendour.* Wheaton, Illinois: The Theosophical Publishing House, 1971.

JONAS, EUGEN, "Fundamentals of Applied Astrology," papers on Scientific Astrology, Bratislava: *Pressfoto,* 1969.

JONES, ERNEST, *On the Nightmare.* New York: Grove Press, 1959.

157

JUNG, CARL G., *Flying Saucers: A Modern Myth of Things Seen in the Sky*. New York: New American Library, 1969.

————, *Man and His Symbols*. New York: Dell, 1968.

————, *Synchronicity*. Princeton: Bollingen Series, Princeton University Press, 1973.

KARAGULLA, S., *Breakthrough to Creativity*. Los Angeles: De Vorss, 1967.

KEEL, JOHN, *Jadoo*. New York: Pyramid Books, 1972.

————, *Our Haunted Planet*. Greenwich, Conn.: Fawcett, 1971.

————, *Strange Creatures from Time and Space*. Greenwich, Conn.: Fawcett, 1970.

KILNER, WALTER J., *The Aura*. New York: Samuel Weiser, 1973.

KLEITMAN, N., "Patterns of Dreaming," *Scientific American*, 203: 1960.

————, *Sleep and Wakefulness*. Chicago: The University of Chicago Press, 1963.

KOESTLER, ARTHUR, *The Act of Creation*. New York: Macmillan, 1964.

————, *The Case of the Midwife Toad*. London: Hutchinson of London, 1971.

————, *The Roots of Coincidence*. London: Hutchinson of London, 1972.

KOZYREV, N., "Possibility of Experimental Study of the Properties of Time," *J P R S, U.S. Dept. of Commerce*, 45238, 2 May 1968.

KRAMER, HEINRICH, AND JAMES SPRENGER, *Malleus Maleficarum*, trans. by Montague Summers. London: Arrow Books, 1971.

KRECHMAL, ARNOLD, "Fire-Walkers of Greece," *Travel*, 108: 1956.

KRIPPNER, STANLEY, and DANIEL RUBIN, eds., *Galaxies of Life: The Human Aura in Acupuncture and Kirlian Photography.* New York: Gordon & Breach, 1973.

KRISHNA, GOPI, *Kundalini: The Evolutionary Energy in Man.* Berkeley, California: Shambala Press, 1971.

KUHN, THOMAS S., *The Structure of Scientific Revolutions.* Chicago: University of Chicago Press, 1962.

KUNZ, GEORGE FREDERICK, *The Curious Lore of Precious Stones.* New York: Dover, 1971.

LAING, R.D., *The Politics of Experience.* New York: Ballantine, 1967.

LAKHOVSKY, GEORGE, *L'origine de la Vie.* Paris: Éditions Nilsson, 1925.

LANGER, SUSANNE K., *Philosophy in a New Key: A Study in the Symbolism of Reason, Rite and Art.* New York: New American Library, n.d.

LANGLEY, NOEL, *Edgar Cayce on Reincarnation.* New York: Paperback Library, 1967.

LASKI, MARGHANITA, *Ecstasy: A Study of Some Secular and Religious Experiences.* London: Cresset Press, 1961.

LAWRENCE, GEORGE L., "Biophysical AV Data Transfer," *AV Communication Review,* 15:2, 1967.

————, "Interstellar Communications Signals," *Information Bulletin No. 72,* San Bernardino, California: Ecola Institute.

————, "Interstellar Communications: What are the Prospects?" *Electronics World,* October 1971.

LAWRENCE, JODI, *Alpha Brainwaves.* New York: Avon Books, 1972.

LAYNE, MEADE, ed., *The Cameron Aurameter.* Vista, California: Borderland Sciences Research Foundation, 1970.

LEADBEATER, C.W. *The Astral Plane.* Wheaton, Illinois: The Theosophical Publishing House, 1968.

————, *The Chakras.* Wheaton, Illinois: The Theosophical Publishing House, 1972.

————, *Man Visible and Invisible.* Wheaton, Illinois: The Theosophical Publishing House, 1971.

LEAVITT, RICHARD T., "To Walk on Fire You Must First Master Yourself," *The New York Times,* April 29, 1973.

LE SHAN, LAWRENCE, *The Medium, the Mystic and the Physicist.* New York: Viking Press, 1974.

LESSA, WILLIAM A. and EVON Z. VOGT, *Reader in Comparative Religion: An Anthropological Approach,* 2nd ed. New York: Harper and Row, 1965.

LETHBRIDGE, T.C., *Ghost and Divining Rod.* London: Routledge & Kegan Paul, 1963.

————, *Ghost and Ghoul.* London: Routledge and Kegan Paul, 1961.

LEWIN, KURT, *A Dynamic Theory of Personality.* New York: McGraw, 1935.

LEWIS, I.M., "The Anthropologist's Encounter With The Supernatural," *Parapsychology Review,* 5:2, 1974.

————, *Ecstatic Religion: An Anthropological Study of Spirit Possession and Shamanism.* Baltimore: Penguin, 1971.

LIEBER, LILLIAN R., and HUGH G., *The Einstein Theory of Relativity: A Trip to the Fourth Dimension.* New York: Holt, Rinehart & Winston, 1945.

LILLY, JOHN C., *Center of the Cyclone.* New York: Julian Press, 1972.

LINDSEY, D., "Common Factors in Sensory Deprivation, Sensory Distortion and Sensory Overload," in P. Solomon et al., *Sensory Deprivation.* Cambridge, Mass.: Harvard University Press, 1961.

LIPPMAN, DEBORAH, and PAUL COLIN, *How to Make Amulets, Charms and Talismans: What They Mean and How to Use Them.* New York: M. Evans and Co., 1974.

LITVAG, IRVING, *Singer in the Shadows.* New York: Popular Library, n.d.

LODGE, SIR OLIVER, *The Survival of Man*. London: Methuen, 1911.

LOEHR, REV. FRANKLIN, *The Power of Prayer on Plants*. New York: Signet Books, 1969.

LONG, CHARLES H., *Alpha: The Myth of Creation*. New York: Collier Books, 1969.

LONG, MAX FREEDOM, *The Secret Science Behind Miracles*. Visa, California: Huna Research Publications, 1948.

LOONEY, DOUGLAS S., "Senility Is Reversible," *Science Digest*, December 1973.

LUCE, GAY GAER, *Body Time*. New York: Bantam Books, 1973.

————, and Julius Segal, *Sleep*. New York: Lancer Books, 1967.

LYTTON, BULWER, *Uril: The Power of the Coming Race*. Blauvelt, New York: Rudolf Steiner Publications, 1972.

MABY, J.C., and P.T. FRANKLIN, *The Physics of the Divining Rod*. London: G. Bell & Sons, 1939.

MACLEAN, GORDON, SR., *Dowsing: An Introduction to an Ancient Practice*. South Portland, Maine: written, reproduced and distributed by Gordon MacLean, Sr., 1971.

MALINOWSKI, BRONISLAW, *Magic, Science and Religion*. New York: Doubleday-Anchor Books, 1948.

Mankind Research Unlimited, Inc., 1325½ Wisconsin Avenue, N.W., Washington, D.C. 20007, "Kirlian" Electrophotography Data Package.

MANN, ALFRED E., "Dr. Velikovsky and Edgar Cayce," *The Searchlight*, 17:6, 1965.

MANN, EDWARD W., *Orgone, Reich and Eros*. New York: Simon & Schuster, 1973.

MASLOW, ABRAHAM, *The Psychology of Science: A Reconnaissance*. Chicago: Henry Regnery, 1969.

MASTER, R., and J. HOUSTON, *The Varieties of Psychedelic Experience*. New York: Holt, Rinehart & Winston, 1966.

161

MATSON, FLOYD W., *The Broken Image*. New York: George Braziller, 1946.

McCREERY, CHARLES, *Psychical Phenomena and the Physical World*. New York: Ballantine, n.d.

MEAD, G.R.S., *The Doctrine of the Subtle Body in Western Tradition*. Wheaton, Illinois: The Theosophical Publishing House, 1967.

The Medical Group, Theosophical Research Centre, London. *The Mystery of Healing*. Wheaton, Illinois: The Theosophical Publishing House, 1968.

MELZACK, RONALD, *The Puzzle of Pain*. Harmondsworth, Middlesex, England: Penguin, 1973.

MENZEL, DONALD H., and LYLE B. BOYD, *The World of Flying Saucers: A Scientific Examination of a Major Myth of the Space Age*. New York: Doubleday, 1963.

MESMER, FRANZ ANTON, *Le Magnetism Animal*. Paris: Payot, 1971.

MÉTRAUX, ALFRED, *Voodoo in Haiti*. New York: Schocken Books, 1972.

MICHEL, AIMÉ, *The Truth About Flying Saucers*. New York: Pyramid, 1967.

MONER, JOHN, *Cells, Their Structure and Function*. Dubuque, Iowa: Wm. C. Brown Co., 1972.

MONOD, JACQUES, *Chance and Necessity*. New York: Alfred A. Knopf, 1971.

MONROE, ROBERT A., *Journeys Out of the Body*. New York: Doubleday-Anchor, 1973.

MUFTIC, MAHMOUD K., *Researches on the Aura Phenomena*. Hastings, England: The Society of Metaphysicians Ltd., 1970.

MULDOON, SYLVAN, and HEREWARD CARRINGTON, *The Case for Astral Projection*. Chicago: Aries Press, 1936 (out of print).

————, *The Projection of the Astral Body*. New York: Samuel Weiser, n.d.

MURPHY, GARDNER, *The Challenge of Psychical Research.* New York: Harper & Row, 1961.

————, and ROBERT O. BALLOU, eds., *William James on Psychical Research.* New York: Viking Press, 1969.

MUSÈS, CHARLES, and ARTHUR M. YOUNG, eds., *Consciousness and Reality.* New York: Outerbridge & Lazard, 1972.

MYERS, F.W.H., *Human Personality and Its Survival of Bodily Death.* New York: University Books, 1961.

NASH, CARROLL B., "Medical Parapsychology," *Parapsychology Review,* 3:1, 1972.

NATHAN, PETER, *The Nervous System.* Baltimore: Penguin Books, n.d.

NAUMOV, E., "From Telepathy to Telekinesis," *Journal of Paraphysics,* 2:2, 1966.

NELSON, J.H., "Planetary Position Effect on Shortwave Signal Quality," *Electrical Engineering,* 71:421, 1952.

————, "Shortwave Radio Propagation Correlation with Planetary Positions," *RCA Review, 12:26,* 1951.

NIXON, FRANCES, *Born to be Magnetic,* Vol. 1. Chemainus, British Columbia: Magnetic Publishers, 1971.

NORMAN, DIANA, *The Stately Ghosts of England.* London: Muller, 1963.

NOVICK, SHELDON, *The Careless Atom.* New York: Delta, n.d.

OESTERREICH, T.K., *Possession: Demoniacal and Other.* New York: University Books, 1966.

ORNSTEIN, ROBERT E., *The Psychology of Consciousness.* New York: Viking Press, 1972.

OSBORN, ARTHUR W., *The Expansion of Awareness: One Man's Search for Meaning in Living.* Wheaton, Illinois: The Theosophical Publishing House, 1967.

————, *The Meaning of Personal Existence: In the Light of Paranormal Phenomena, Reincarnation and Mystical Experience.* Wheaton, Illinois: The Theosophical Publishing House, 1968.

163

OSBORN, CLIFFORD W., *The Future is Now: The Significance of Precognition.* New York: University Books, 1961.

OSIS, KARLIS, *Deathbed Observations by Physicians and Nurses.* New York: Parapsychology Foundation, Monograph No. 3, 1961.

————, "ESP Over Distance: Research on the ESP Channel," *Journal of the American Society for Physical Research*, 29: 1965.

————, "ESP Over Distance: A Survey of Experiments Published in English," *Journal of the American Society for Psychical Research*, 59:1, 1965.

OSTRANDER, SHEILA, and LYNN SCHROEDER, *Astrological Birth Control.* Englewood Cliffs, New Jersey: Prentice-Hall, 1972.

————, *Handbook of PSI Discoveries.* New York: Berkley Publishing Corp., 1974.

————, *Psychic Discoveries Behind the Iron Curtain.* Englewood Cliffs, New Jersey: Prentice-Hall, 1971.

OTT, JOHN N., *Health and the Light—The Effects of Natural and Artifical Light on Man and Other Living Things.* Old Greenwich, Conn.: Devin-Adair, 1973.

OUSELEY, L.G.J., *The Science of the Aura.* London: L.N. Fowler & Co., 1949.

OUSPENSKY, P.D., *A New Model of the Universe.* New York: Vintage Books, 1971.

————, *The Psychology of Man's Possible Evolution.* New York: Alfred A. Knopf, 1969.

OWEN, A.R.G., *Can We Explain the Poltergeist?* New York: Garrett Publications, 1964.

————, "A Demonstration of Voluntary Psychokinesis: Report of a Study," *New Horizons*, 1:1, 1972.

————, "Experiments on ESP in Relation to (a) Distance and (b) Mood and Subject Matter," *New Horizons*, 1:2, 1973.

————, "Generation of an 'Aura': A New Parapsychological Phenomenon," *New Horizons*, 1:1, 1972.

————, and G.A.V. MORGAN, "The 'Rim' Aura: An Optical

Illusion: A Genuine but Non-Psychic Perception," *New Horizons*, 1:3, 1974.

———— and V. SIMS, *Science and the Spook*. London: Dennis Dobson, 1971.

PANCHADASI, SWAMI, *The Human Aura: Astrol Colors and Thought Forms*. Hackensack, New Jersey: Wehman Bros., 1940.

Parapsychological Association, *Techniques and Status of Modern Parapsychology*. First Symposium, presented at the 137th annual meeting of the American Association for the Advancement of Science. Chicago, Illinois: December 27, 1970.

PAUWELS, LOUIS, and JACQUES BERGIER, *Impossible Possibilities*. New York: Stein & Day, 1971.

————, *The Morning of the Magicians*. New York: Stein & Day, 1963.

PAYNE, BURYL, *Getting There Without Drugs: Techniques and Theories for the Expansion of Consciousness*. New York: Viking, 1973.

PAYNE, PHOEBE D., and LAURENCE J. BENDIT, *This World and That: An Analytical Study of Psychic Communication*. Wheaton, Illinois: The Theosophical Publishing House, 1969.

PEARCE, JOSEPH CHILTON, *The Crack in the Cosmic Egg: Challenging Constructs of Mind and Reality*. New York: Pocket Books, 1973.

PEARCE-HIGGINS, J.D. CANON, and REV. G. STANLEY WHITBY, eds., *Life, Death and Psychical Research: Studies on Behalf of the Churches' Fellowship for Psychical and Spiritual Studies*. London: Rider & Co., 1973.

PELTON, ROBERT W., *The Complete Book of Voodoo*. New York: Berkley Publishing Corp., 1973.

PENFIELD, W., and L. ROBERTS, *Speech and Brain Mechanisms*. Princeton, New Jersey: Princeton University Press, 1959.

Pensée, Special Issue on Immanuel Velikovsky, "How Much of Yesterday's Heresy is Today's Science?" 2:2, 1972.

PICCARDI, G., *The Chemical Basis of Medical Climatology*. Springfield, Illinois: Charles Thomas, 1962.

PIERRAKOS, JOHN C., *The Energy Field in Man and Nature.* New York: Institute of Bioenergetic Analysis, 1971.

PODMORE, FRANK, *From Mesmer to Christian Science.* New York: University Books, 1963.

POPLE, J., "A Theory on the Structure of Water," *Proceedings of the Royal Society,* A202:323, 1950.

POWELL, ARTHUR E., *The Astral Body.* Wheaton, Illinois: The Theosophical Publishing House, 1973.

_____, *The Etheric Double.* London: The Theosophical Publishing House, 1969.

POYNTON, JOHN, "Parapsychology and the Biological Sciences," *Parapsychology Review,* 4:2, 1973.

PRAT, S., and J. SCHLEMMER, "Electrography," *Journal of the Biological Photographic Association,* 7: 1939.

PRESMAN, A.S. *Electromagnetic Fields of Life.* New York: Plenum Press, 1970.

PRIESTLEY, J.B., *Man and Time.* New York: Crescent, n.d.

Probe—The Unknown, A Special Report on UFO's. Spring 1974.

PSALTIS, LINA, ed., *Dynamics of the Psychic World: Comments by H.P. Blavatsky.* Wheaton, Illinois: The Theosophical Publishing House, 1972.

Psychic Observer: *Journal of Spiritual Science,* a Special Issue on Eloptic Energy, 33:3, 1972.

Psychic Observer: *Journal of Spiritual Science,* a Special Issue on Radiesthesia, 32:1, 1971.

PUHARICH, ANDRIJA, *Beyond Telepathy.* New York: Doubleday, 1962.

_____, *The Sacred Mushroom: Key to the Door of Eternity.* New York: Doubleday, 1959.

_____, *Uri: A Journal of the Mystery of Uri Geller.* New York: Doubleday, 1974.

PUTMAN, J.L., *Isotopes,* rev. ed. Baltimore: Pelican, 1965.

166

RAKNES, OLA. *Wilhelm Reich and Orgonomy: The Controversial Theory of Life Energy.* Baltimore: Pelican, 1971.

RAO, K. RAMAKRISHNA, *Experimental Parapsychology: A Review and Interpretation.* Springfield, Illinois: Charles Thomas, 1966.

RAUDIVE, K., *Breakthrough.* New York: Taplinger, 1971.

RAVENSCROFT, TREVOR, *The Spear of Destiny.* London: Neville Spearman, 1972.

RAVITZ, LEONARD J., "Electromagnetic Field Monitoring of Changing State-Function, Including Hypnotic States," *Journal of the American Society of Psychosomatic Dentistry and Medicine,* 17: 1970.

———— , "Periodic Changes in Electromagnetic Fields," *Annals of the New York Academy of Science,* 96:1181, 1960.

RAWSON, PHILIP, and LASZLO LEGEZA, *Tao: The Chinese Philosophy of Time and Change.* London: Thames and Hudson, 1973.

RECHNITZ, KURT, "The Significance of Lunar Phases Theory for the Regulation of Conception," Chapters on Scientific Astrology, Bratislava: *Pressfoto,* 1969.

REGUSH, JUNE and NICHOLAS M., eds., *Psi: The Other World Catalogue.* New York: G.P. Putnam's Sons, 1974.

REGUSH, NICHOLAS M., ed., *The Human Aura.* New York: Berkley Publishing Corp., 1974.

———— , ed., *Visibles and Invisibles: A Primer for a New Sociological Imagination.* Boston: Little, Brown, 1973.

REICH, WILHELM, *The Cancer Biopathy.* New York: Orgone Institute Press, 1948.

———— , *Ether, God and Devil and Cosmic Superimposition.* New York: Farrar, Straus and Giroux, 1973.

RETALLACK, DOROTHY, *The Sound of Music and Plants.* Santa Monica, California: DeVorss & Co., 1973.

REYES, BENITO F., *Scientific Evidence of the Existence of the*

Soul. Wheaton, Illinois: The Theosophical Publishing House, 1970.

REZNIKOFF, MARVIN, "Psychological Factors in Breast Cancer: A Preliminary Study of Some Personality Trends in Cancer of the Breast," *Psychosomatic Medicine,* 27:2, 1955.

RHINE, J.B., *The Reach of the Mind.* New York: William Sloane Association, 1947.

RHINE, LOUISA E., *ESP in Life and Lab: Tracing Hidden Channels.* New York: Collier Books, 1969.

————, *Mind Over Matter.* London: Macmillan, 1970.

ROBERTS, JANE, *The Education of Oversoul 7.* Englewood Cliffs, New Jersey: Prentice-Hall, 1973.

————, *The Seth Material.* Englewood Cliffs, New Jersey: Prentice-Hall, 1970.

————, *Seth Speaks: The Eternal Validity of the Soul.* Englewood Cliffs, New Jersey: Prentice-Hall, 1972.

ROBERTS, URSULA, *The Mystery of the Human Aura.* London: The Spiritualist Association of Great Britain, 1972.

ROBINSON, LYTLE, *Edgar Cayce's Story of the Origin and Destiny of Man.* New York: Coward, McCann & Geoghegan, 1972.

ROCARD, Y., *Le Signal du Sorcier.* Paris: Dunod, 1963.

ROLL, WILLIAM G., *The Poltergeist.* New York: New American Library, 1974.

RONY, JEROME-ANTOINE, *A History of Magic.* New York: Tower Publications, n.d.

RORVIK, DAVID M., "Jack Schwarz Feels No Pain," *Esquire,* December 1973.

ROSE, LOUIS, *Faith Healing,* rev. ed. Baltimore: Penguin, 1971.

ROSENTHAL, ROBERT, *Experimenter Effects in Behavioral Research.* New York: Appleton-Century-Crofts, 1966.

Rosicrucian Wisdom Teachings, *The Mystery of the Human Aura.* New York: Society of Rosicrucians Inc., 1950.

168

RUDHYAR, DANE, *The Planetarization of Consciousness: From the Individual to the Whole.* New York: Harper & Row, 1972.

RUPPELT, EDWARD J., *The Report on Unidentified Flying Objects.* New York: Ace Books, n.d.

RUSSELL, EDWARD W., *Design for Destiny.* London: Neville Spearman, 1971.

————, *Report on Radionics.* London: Neville Spearman, 1973.

RYZL, MILAN, *Parapsychology: A Scientific Approach.* New York: Hoffman Books, 1970.

SAGAN, CARL, ed., *Communication with Extraterrestrial Intelligence.* Cambridge, Massachusetts: MIT Press, 1973.

————, *The Cosmic Connection: An Extraterrestrial Perspective.* New York: Doubleday, 1973.

ST. CLAIR, DAVID, *Drum and Candle.* New York: Doubleday, 1971.

SANDERSON, IVAN T., *Invisible Residents.* New York: Avon, 1973.

————, *Uninvited Visitors.* London: Neville Spearman, 1969.

SARGANT, WILLIAM, *The Mind Possessed: A Physiology of Possession, Mysticism and Faith Healing.* Philadelphia: J.B. Lippincott, 1974.

SCHAFFRANKE, ROLF, "Secrets of the Human Aura," *Fate Magazine,* 17:6, 1964.

SCHLEICHER, CARL. "Some Evidence for Dowsing—A Mythological Approach," *Mankind Research Unlimited* paper. Washington, D.C., 1973.

SCHMIDT, H., "Mental Influence on Random Events," *New Scientist,* 50:757, 1971.

SCHNECK, HAROLD M., *Immunology: The Double-Edged Sword.* New York: George Braziller, 1974.

SCHNEER, CECIL J., *Mind and Matter: Man's Changing Concept of the Material World.* New York: Grove Press, 1970.

SCHUL, BILL D., "The Link," *Probe—The Unknown*. December 1973.

SCHULMAN, ARNOLD, *Baba*. New York: Pocket Books, 1973.

SCHWARTZ, STEPHAN, and JAMES BOLEN, "Interview: Ambrose and Olga Worrall," *Psychic*. March-April, 1972.

Scientific American, Special Issue on Medicine, "Life and Death and Medicine," 229:3, 1973.

SEABROOK, WILLIAM, *Magic Island*. New York: Harcourt, 1929.

SECHRIST, ELSIE, *Dreams: Your Magic Mirror*. New York: Dell, 1969.

SELIGMANN, KURT, *Magic, Supernaturalism and Religion*. New York: Pantheon Books, 1949.

SELIGMAN, MARTIN E.P., "Submissive Death: Giving up on Life," *Psychology Today*, May 1974.

SEXTUS, CARL, *Hypnotism: A Correct Guide to the Science and How Subjects Are Influenced*. North Hollywood, California: Wilshire Book Co., 1971.

SHAH, IDRIES, *Oriental Magic*. London: Octagon, 1968.

_____, *The Way of the Sufi*. New York: Dutton, 1970.

SHAPIRO, BETTY, "Magician Debunks Parapsychology," *The Gazette*, March 21, 1973.

_____, "Parapsychology: One Way to Unravel Mysteries of Life?" *The Gazette*, March 12, 1973.

SHERMAN, HAROLD and SIR HUBERT WILKINS, *Thoughts Through Space*. Greenwich, Conn.: Fawcett Publications, 1973.

SHKLOVSKII, I.S., AND CARL SAGAN, *Intelligent Life in the Universe*. New York: Delta, 1966.

SHURÉ, EDOUARD, *From Sphinx to Christ: An Occult History*. Blauvelt, New York: Rudolf Steiner Publications, 1970.

SILVERBERG, ROBERT, *Lost Cities and Vanished Civilizations*. New York: Bantam, 1963.

_____, *The Mound Builders*. New York: Ballantine, 1974.

170

SIMEONS, A.T.W., *Man's Presumptuous Brain*. New York: E.T. Dutton & Co., 1962.

SIMON, MORRIS, "Truth-Finding Trial by Poison," *Probe—The Unknown*, June 1973.

SINCLAIR, UPTON, *Mental Radio: An Amazing Series of Extrasensory Events*. New York: Collier Books, 1971.

SIU, R.G.H., *The Tao of Science*. Cambridge, Massachusetts: MIT Press, 1957.

SMITH, SUSY, *The Enigma of Out-of-Body Travel*. New York: New American Library, 1968.

SMITH, WARREN, "The Behind-the-Headlines Story of the Pascagoula UFO Kidnap," *Saga*, March 1974.

SMYTHIES, J.R., "The Mind-Brain Problem Today: A Viewpoint from the Neurosciences," *Parapsychology Review*, 4:2, 1973.

SOAL, S.G. and F. BATEMAN, *Modern Experiments in Telepathy*. London: Faber & Faber, 1954.

SPENCE, LEWIS, *An Encyclopedia of Occultism*. Secaucus, New Jersey: Citadel Press, 1974.

SPERRY, R.W., "The Eye and the Brain," *Scientific American*, offprint No. 1090.

————, "Neurology and the Mind-Brain Problem," *American Scientist*, 40: 1951.

SPRAGGETT, ALLEN with WILLIAM V. RAUSCHER, *Arthur Ford: The Man Who Talked with the Dead*. New York: New American Library, 1974.

————, *Probing the Unexplained*. New York: World Publishing Co., 1971.

STANFORD, RAY, "Teleporting a Meteorite," *Psychic*, September-October 1973.

STEARN, JESS, *Edgar Cayce—The Sleeping Prophet*. New York: Doubleday, 1967.

————, *A Time for Astrology*. New York: New American Library, 1972.

171

STECKER, FLOYD W., "The Role of Antimatter in Big-Bang Cosmology," *Science and Public Affairs,* January 1974.

STEIGER, BRAD, *Atlantis Rising.* New York: Dell, 1973.

————, *Medicine Power: The American Indian's Revival of His Spiritual Heritage and Its Relevance for Modern Man.* New York: Doubleday, 1974.

————, *The Psychic Feats of Olof Jonsson.* New York: Popular Library, n.d.

————, *Revelation: The Divine Fire.* Englewood Cliffs, New Jersey: Prentice-Hall, 1973.

————, *Strange Guests.* New York: Ace, n.d.

STEINER, RUDOLF, *Cosmic Memory: Atlantis and Lemuria.* Blauvelt, New York: Rudolf Steiner Publications, 1959.

STEVENSON, IAN, "The Evidence for Survival from Claimed Memories of Former Incarnations" (monograph). Surrey, England: M.C. Peto, 1961.

————, *Telepathic Impressions: A Review and Report of Thirty-Five New Cases.* Charlottesville: University Press of Virginia, 1970.

STRÖMBERG, GUSTAF, *The Soul of the Universe.* North Hollywood, California: Educational Research Institute, 1965.

STRONG, L.C., *Biological Aspects of Cancer and Aging.* New York: Pergamon, 1968.

SUMMERS, MONTAGUE, *The Geography of Witchcraft.* New York: University Books, 1958.

————, *The History of Witchcraft and Demonology.* London: Routledge & Kegan Paul, 1973.

Sunday Times Supplement, "The Great Bordeaux Magnetic Machine Mystery," January 7, 1973.

SUTHERLAND, JAMES, "Ghost Universe," *Vertex,* 2:2, 1974.

Symposium of Psychotronics, Part II: Anisotropy, *Journal of Paraphysics.* 5:3, 1971.

172

_____, Part III: Seminar on Bioplasm, *Journal of Paraphysics*, 5:4, 1971.

SZASZ, THOMAS S., *Ideology and Insanity: Essays on the Psychiatric Dehumanization of Man*. New York: Doubleday & Co., 1970.

TAFF, BARRY E., "Brain Holograms: The Light Within," *Probe— The Unknown* 1:6, 1973.

TANAGRAS, A., "Psychophysical Elements in Parapsychological Traditions." *Parapsychological Monographs No. 7*, New York: Parapsychology Foundation, 1967.

TANNER, FLORICE, *The Mystery Teachings in World Religions*. Wheaton, Illinois: The Theosophical Publishing House, 1973.

TANSLEY, DAVID V., *Radionics: And the Subtle Anatomy of Man*. Rustington, Sussex, England: Health Science Press, 1972.

TART, CHARLES T., ed., *Altered States of Consciousness*. New York: Doubleday, 1972.

_____, "The Scientific Study of the Human Aura," *Journal of the Society for Psychical Research*, 46:751, 1972.

TCHIJEWSKY, A.L., "L'action de l'activité périodique solaire sur les phénomènes sociaux," *Trait de Climatologie Biologique et Medicale*. Paris: Masson, 1934.

THOMAS, LEWIS, *The Lives of a Cell*. New York: Viking, 1974.

THOMPSON, WILLIAM IRWIN, *At the Edge of History*. New York: Harper & Row, 1971.

TIETZE, THOMAS R., "Psychical Research in America: The Early Years," *Psychic*, November-December, 1970.

TILLER, WILLIAM A., "Are Psychoenergetic Pictures Possible?" *New Scientist*, 62:895, 1974.

_____, "Radionics, Radiesthesia and Physics," *Proceedings of the Academy of Parapsychology and Medicine*, A Symposium on the varieties of healing experience, 1971.

_____, "A Technical Report on Some Psychoenergetic Devices," *A.R.E. Journal*, 7: 1972.

173

TOMLINSON, H., *The Divination of Disease: A Study in Radiesthesia.* Wayside, England: Health Science Press, n.d.

TOMPKINS, PETER, *Secrets of the Great Pyramid.* New York: Harper & Row, 1971.

————, and CHRISTOPHER BIRD, *The Secret Life of Plants.* New York: Harper & Row, 1973.

TORREY, E. FULLER, *The Mind Game: Witch Doctors and Psychiatrists.* New York: Bantam, 1973.

TRINDER, W.H., *Dowsing.* London: G. Bell & Sons, 1967.

TROMP, A., "Review of the Possible Physiological Causes of Dowsing," *International Journal of Parapsychology,* 10:4, 1968.

TROTTER, ROBERT J., and LISE J. SHAWVER, "The Mysterious Powers of Uri Geller," *Human Behavior,* February 1974.

TURNER, GORDON, *An Outline of Spiritual Healing.* New York: Warner Paperback Library, 1972.

TWITCHELL, PAUL, *Eckankar.* New York: Lancer Books, 1969.

TYLOR, SIR EDWARD BURNETT, *Religion in Primitive Culture* (Part 2 of *Primitive Culture*). New York: Harper & Brothers, 1958.

TYRRELL, G.N.M. *Apparitions.* New York: University Books, 1961.

————, *The Personality of Man.* Baltimore: Penguin, 1947.

ULLMAN, MONTAGUE, and STANLEY KRIPPNER, *Dream Studies and Telepathy: An Experimental Approach.* New York: Parapsychological Monograph No. 12, Parapsychology Foundation, 1970.

————, with ALAN VAUGHAN, *Dream Telepathy.* New York: Macmillan, 1973.

UNDERWOOD, PETER, *Gazetteer of British Ghosts.* London: Souvenir Press, 1971.

VALENTINE, TOM, *Psychic Surgery.* Chicago: Henry Regnery, 1973.

VALLÉE, JACQUES, *Anatomy of a Phenomenon: Unidentified*

Objects in Space—A Scientific Appraisal. Chicago: Henry Regnery Co., 1965.

————, "UFO's: The Psychic Component," *Psychic,* January-February 1974.

VAN DUSEN, WILSON, *The Natural Depth in Man.* New York: Harper & Row, 1972.

VAN OVER, RAYMOND, ed., *Psychology and Extrasensory Perception.* New York: New American Library, 1972.

VASILIEV, L.L., *Experiments in Mental Suggestion.* Hampshire, England: Galley Hill Press, 1963.

VAUGHAN, ALAN, *Patterns of Prophecy.* New York: Hawthorn, 1973.

————, "Poltergeist Investigations in Germany," *Psychic,* March-April 1970.

VELIKOVSKY, IMMANUEL, *Ages in Chaos: A Reconstruction of Ancient History from the Exodus to King Akhnaton.* New York: Doubleday & Co., 1952.

————, *Earth in Upheaval.* New York: Dell, 1968.

————, *Worlds in Collision.* New York: Dell, 1967.

VOGEL, VIRGIL J., *American Indian Medicine.* New York: Ballantine, 1973.

VON DÄNIKEN, ERICH, *Chariots of the Gods?* New York: Bantam Books, 1971.

————, *Gods from Outer Space.* New York: Bantam Books, 1972.

————, *The Gold of the Gods.* London: Souvenir Press, 1973.

VON REICHENBACH, KARL, *The Odic Force: Letters on Od and Magnetism.* New York: University Books, 1968.

WAGNER, HENRY N., *Principles of Nuclear Medicine.* Philadelphia: W.B. Saunders Co., 1968.

WAITE, ARTHUR E., *The Book of Ceremonial Magic.* New York: University Books, 1961.

175

WALKER, KENNETH, *The Extra-Sensory Mind.* New York: Harper & Row, 1972.

WARD, RITCHIE R., *The Living Clock.* New York: New American Library, 1972.

WATERS, FRANK, *Book of the Hopi.* New York: Ballantine Books, 1969.

WATSON, J.D., *The Double Helix.* New York: Atheneum Publishers, 1968.

WATSON, LYALL, *Supernature.* New York: Doubleday, 1973.

WATTS, ALAN W., *The Joyous Cosmology.* New York: Vintage Books, 1962.

WEIL, ANDREW, *The Natural Mind: A New Way of Looking at Drugs and the Higher Consciousness.* Boston, Houghton Mifflin Co., 1973.

WELLMAN, ALICE, *Spirit Magic.* New York: Berkley Publishing Corp., 1973.

WEST, JOHN ANTHONY, and JAN GERHARD TOONER, *The Case for Astrology.* Harmondsworth, Middlesex, England: 1973.

WESTLAKE, AUBREY T., *The Pattern of Health: A Search for a Greater Understanding of the Life Force in Health and Disease.* London: V. Stuart, 1961.

WETHERED, VERNON, *An Introduction to Medical Radiesthesia and Radionics.* London: C.W. Daniel, 1974.

————, *The Practice of Medical Radiesthesia.* London: L.N. Fowler & Co., 1967.

WHITE, GEORGE STARR, *The Story of the Human Aura.* Mokelumne Hill, California: Health Research, 1969.

WHITE, JOHN W., "Exobiology: The Study of Extraterrestrial Life," *Psychic*, March-April 1973.

————, ed., *The Highest State of Consciousness.* New York: Doubleday & Co., 1972.

————, ed., *What Is Meditation?* New York: Doubleday, 1974.

WHITE, STEWART EDWARD, *The Betty Book*. New York: E.P. Dutton & Co., 1937.

————, *The Unobstructed Universe*. New York: Macmillan, 1925.

WHITEHEAD, ALFRED N., *Science and the Modern World*. New York: Macmillan, 1925.

WHITROW, G.J., *What Is Time?* London: Thames & Hudson, 1972.

WILHELM, RICHARD, trans., *The Secret of the Golden Flower*, rev. ed. London: Routledge & Kegan Paul, 1962.

WILLIAMS, ROGER J. *Nutrition Against Disease*. New York: Bantam Books, 1973.

WILSON, COLIN, *The Occult*. New York: Vintage Books, 1973.

WOODS, WILLIAM, *A History of the Devil*. New York: G.P. Putnam's Sons, 1974.

WOODWARD, MARY ANN, *Edgar Cayce's Story of Karma*. New York: Berkley Publishing Corp., 1972.

WORRALL, AMBROSE A., and OLGA N., with WILL OURSLER. *Explore Your Psychic World*. New York: Harper & Row, 1970.

WOSIEN, MARIA-GABRIELE, *Sacred Dance: Encounter With the Gods*. London: Thames and Hudson, 1974.

WRAY, JAMES G., "Edgar Cayce and Space-Time," *ARE Journal*, 8:6, 1973.

WRENCH, G.T., *The Wheel of Health: The Sources of Long Life and Health Among the Hunza*. New York: Schocken Books, 1972.

YOGANANDA PARAMAHANSA, Autobiography of a Yogi. New York: The Philosophical Library, 1946.

ZUBEK, JOHN T., ed., *Sensory Deprivation, Fifteen Years of Research*. New York: Appleton-Century-Crofts, 1969.

Index

179

181